T0271077

Information Economics with Real Estate Applications

Information Economics with Real Estate Applications provides the reader with an academic toolkit to understand strategic interactions of individuals and companies in a world of scarce resources and asymmetric information. Beyond theoretical frameworks and models, examples in the real estate and construction industry are used to illustrate the practical relevance of the concepts discussed.

Property developers, brokers, construction firms and investment managers – as individuals or companies – make decisions in response to their clients', customers' and partners' behaviours. To align conflicting interests and achieve optimal outcomes for individuals, companies and society at large, those interactions need to be governed efficiently. Using models from microeconomics and contract theory, this book helps the reader to analyse the complex relations between different industry stakeholders from the perspective of markets and organisations.

Although it mainly targets students at the Masters or PhD level in real estate or similar subjects without previous knowledge in information economics, the general theory presented should be of interest to any student who wants an introductory text in information economics. At the same time, by building upon real-world examples, the book allows industry practitioners to reflect on and optimise their strategic decision-making in a more structured way.

Fredrik Armerin has a PhD in Mathematical Statistics from KTH Royal Institute of Technology, and a licentiate degree in Real Estate and Construction Management, also from KTH Royal Institute of Technology. He is a Fellow of The Institute of Mathematics and its Applications.

Madeleine Hoeft is a commercial asset manager in a global real estate investment firm in Frankfurt, Germany. She has an academic background in Real Estate and Construction Management (MSc) from KTH Royal Institute of Technology, National University of Singapore and Stanford University, and has gained professional experience in the field of property and asset management, transaction advisory and construction project management.

Information Economics with Real Estate Applications

Fredrik Armerin and Madeleine Hoeft

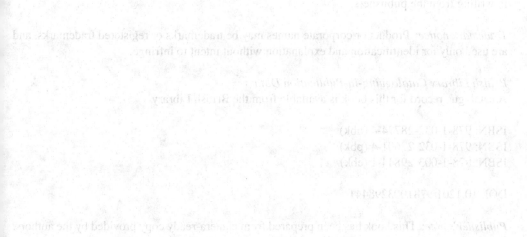

Routledge
Taylor & Francis Group

LONDON AND NEW YORK

Designed cover image: © Getty Images

First published 2023
by Routledge
4 Park Square, Milton Park, Abingdon, Oxon OX14 4RN

and by Routledge
605 Third Avenue, New York, NY 10158

Routledge is an imprint of the Taylor & Francis Group, an informa business

British Library Cataloguing-in-Publication Data
A catalogue record for this book is available from the British Library

ISBN: 978-1-032-28774-4 (hbk)
ISBN: 978-1-032-27601-4 (pbk)
ISBN: 978-1-003-29844-1 (ebk)

DOI: 10.1201/9781003298441

Publisher's note: This book has been prepared from camera-ready copy provided by the authors.

Contents

List of Figures

List of Notation

a	Action
α	Constant defining a contract
AC	Average cost
AVC	Average variable cost
β	Constant defining a contract
B	Amount of a "bad"
c	Constant marginal cost in oligopoly models
c_H, c_L	Cost of education in the Spence signalling model
C	Cost function or a constant cost
CS	Consumer's or consumers' surplus
CE	Certainty equivalent
δ	Discount factor
Δ	Difference operator
D	Demand function
DWL	Dead weight loss
E	Expected value
e	Effort
ε	Price elasticity of demand
η	Price elasticity of supply
F	Fixed cost
f	Production function
G	Amount of "good"
k, k_0	Sunk cost
K	Capital
L	Labour
MC	Marginal cost
MC^p	Private marginal cost
MC^s	The society's marginal cost.
n	Number of consumers or number of firms
P	Probability
p	Price
π	Profit
PS	Producer's or producers' surplus
q	Quantity of a good
Q	Total quantity
Q_M	Quantity produced by a monoploy
ρ	Constant absolute coefficient risk aversion
r	Interest rate
r_A	Coefficient of absolute risk aversion
R	Reaction funtion

s	Payment to agent
S	Supply function
s_i	Market share of firm i
σ	Standard deviation
σ^2	Variance
T	Tax or time
u, U	Utility functions
$\overline{U}$	Constant level of utility
VC	Variable cost
w	Wage
w_H, w_L	Wages in a signalling model
W	Welfare
x, y, z	Consumption bundles
x_i	Amount consumed of good i
x_A, x_B	Payoff to Player A and B respectively
X, Y, Z	Random variables or random payoffs
y, y^*, y_H, y_L	Levels of education in the Spence signalling model

Preface

Stakeholders in the built environment such as property developers, brokers, construction firms or investment managers do not act in an isolated fashion, but as part of a larger ecosystem. Individuals, companies and industries therefore need to take several factors and different types of information into account when making strategic decisions in response to their direct clients', customers' and partners' behaviours. As such, they are inevitably linked to each other, both in informal and formal ways. The characteristics of these links determine how the actors choose to interact with each other in order to reach their goals in the light of conflicting interests, scarce resources and asymmetric information. It is therefore crucial to govern these interactions efficiently to reach optimal outcomes for individuals, companies and society at large.

Using the theoretical background of microeconomics and contract theory, this book provides a structure to analyse and understand the interactions of different stakeholders in real estate and construction. It combines academic frameworks with real-world examples to emphasise the direct applicability of the concepts discussed. Although the intended audience of the book is students at the master or PhD level in real estate, property management and similar subjects without any previous knowledge in information economics, the general theory presented should be of interest to any student in economics and finance who wants an introductory text in information economics. By building upon real-world examples, the book allows industry practitioners to reflect on and optimise their business strategies in a more structured way. For a general overview, the connections between the chapters are outlined in Figure 1. Detailed descriptions of the different chapters follow in the next section.

Throughout, we use *models* in order to explain and understand a specific economic situation. There has been a critique against the use of mathematical models in economics, and specifically the use of highly advanced mathematics. We use basic algebra, calculus and probability theory, because we believe it is the best way of describing and analysing economic situations. Nevertheless, remember that every model is an imperfect description of reality. For more on the usefulness of models in economics, see Rodrik [45].

Part I – Foundations

The first part of the book will give the reader the theoretical foundations and notations needed for this book. The two main building blocks are microeconomics and game theory. In Chapter 1, we discuss the basic characteristics of markets and the actors involved. In this context, we illustrate what motivates the actions of different stakeholders in the built environment such as apartment buyers or property developers. In Chapter 2, the fundamentals of game theory are presented. Like microeconomics, game theory is naturally present in business situations and helps to reflect on strategic decision-making such as in lease negotiations or large-scale industry transformations.

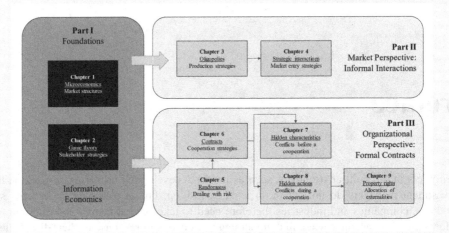

Figure 1: Outline of the book.

Part II – Market Perspective: Informal Interactions

The second part looks at informal interactions between companies from a market perspective. Here, companies are seen as profit-maximising objects, who base their strategies on other players' (expected) actions, consumer demand and internal capacities. The most common market form in which such behaviour can be witnessed are oligopolies. They combine microeconomic concepts with game theory and are central to the analyses and examples in this part of the book. Chapter 3 introduces different form of oligopolies to answer how different firms, e.g., construction equipment providers or real estate developers, should structure their product or service offerings in relation to their competitors. The focus here is mainly on existing market actors and their interactions. In contrast, Chapter 4 focuses on market entry strategies. Using the example of shopping malls, it is shown how companies can enter a new market and how they can prevent their competitors from doing so.

Part III – Organisational Perspective: Formal Contracts

As an alternative to the perspective in Part II, we can look upon a firm as a "nexus of contracts". Here, the firm is a legal entity that enters into formal agreement (i.e., contracts) with its managers, employees, customers and shareholders. This is described in models of information economics, focusing on information about actions of different parties. The contracts between two parties are sets of rules that regulate how the outcome of an economic situation is to be shared between the parties. Often, the set-up includes a principal (a company's board, a property developer, ...) hiring an agent (a CEO, a contractor, ...) to perform a task. In many of these situations, information is not fully transparent and only partially available to the different parties. The outcome of the agent's work can be observed by the principal, while the action or the effort of the agent are unobservable (the "principal-agent relationship"). This is not negative *per se* but can become problematic if one of the parties uses the asymmetric information to gain economic advantage by showing opportunistic behaviour. In Chapter 5, the concept of randomness is introduced. This is essential to understand why information asymmetry and a lack of transparency can cause conflicts in business relationships. It further explains how tasks and risks should best be allocated to achieve efficient outcomes in a collaboration, e.g., when engaging a broker to market a property. Chapter 6 builds on this by explaining the nature of principal-agent relationships in detail. It discusses the role of contracts in an industry context and illustrates, why and under which conditions, different stakeholders collaborate. It also introduces the various conflict potentials and inefficiencies of such a relationship, namely hidden characteristics and hidden actions. Chapter 7 focuses on hidden characteristics, the resulting inefficiencies and potential ways to mitigate them before agreeing to a contract. This concerns for example the selection of service providers, the investment into real assets like buildings or infrastructure as well as the structuring of property insurances. Hidden characteristics also exist within a company, for instance when hiring employees. Chapter 8 addresses the challenges after agreeing to a contract such as how to avoid moral hazard and incentivise the parties to perform to their best ability. Various ways of dealing with these risks are explained and illustrated in the context of property valuation, construction and facility management. Last but not least, Chapter 9 shows how contracts and clearly defined power and control further support efficient interactions of different industry stakeholders in the best societal interest. It discusses property rights in detail and refers to the theoretical foundations of welfare introduced in Part I.

Acknowledgements

We thank Marianne Pieper for her careful revision of the manuscript draft. Students in the MSc course "Contract Theory with Applications to Property Management" at KTH Royal Institute of Technology in Spring 2022 have also contributed to the improvement of the manuscript.

Contributors

Fredrik Armerin has a PhD in Mathematical Statistics from KTH Royal Institute of Technology, and a licenciate degree in Real Estate and Construction Management, also from KTH Royal Institute of Technology. He is a Fellow of The Institute of Mathematics and its Applications.

Madeleine Hoeft is a commercial asset manager in a global real estate investment firm in Frankfurt, Germany. She has an academic background in Real Estate and Construction Management (MSc) from KTH Royal Institute of Technology, National University of Singapore and Stanford University, and has gained professional experience in the field of property and asset management, transaction advisory and construction project management.

Part I

Foundations

Chapter 1

Basic microeconomics

In this chapter, the basic characteristics of markets and their main actors – consumers and producers – are introduced. In addition, the implications for society at large from a welfare perspective are highlighted. It is illustrated what motivates the actions of different stakeholders in the built environment such as apartment buyers or property developers.

Economics can in one sentence be described as finding the efficient use of scarce resources. Since the budget of consumers, the material available to firms and the land on which it is possible to build all are finite, we must find ways to optimally allocate those resources.

1.1 Introduction

After the 2008 financial crisis and in the light of low interest rates, real assets once again became an attractive investment opportunity to private and professional actors. In 2021, the commercial real estate sector in Europe was estimated at approximately 9 trillion US dollars. Especially asset classes such as logistics properties and infrastructure rose in investors' favours in Europe, while the appetite for offices and retail buildings decreased following the Corona pandemic in 2019.[1] The market value of residential real estate with about 24.9 trillion EUR in 2019 was even more significant.[2] In this context, microeconomic theory, as opposed to macroeconomics, studies how individuals and firms allocate their resources and consumption in single markets. We refer to it to understand which factors drive economic behaviour and which actions are required to gain a competitive (often financial) advantage among market participants. Questions addressed from a microeconomic standpoint in this chapter are for example: How does an apartment buyer make an investment decision? How can property developers allocate their resources? And, is an individual actor's optimal action also in the best interest of the society?

1.2 Consumers

1.2.1 Preferences

As a consumer approaches a shop or market square in order to decide what to buy, chooses among which education to attend or which house or apartment to buy, the choices are ruled by, among

---

[1]https://www.statista.com/statistics/1096511/share-of-real-estate-investment-europe-by-sector/
[2]http://www.europeanrealestateforum.eu/key-facts/

other things, the consumer's *preferences*. By "consumer" we mean any economic entity that can buy goods in a market. Examples include individuals, firms and governments. Note that different consumers can have, and in general do have, different preferences. In order to formalise how the preferences determine which goods are being bought by a consumer, we introduce some notation. A *consumption bundle x* is an n-dimensional vector $x = (x_1, x_2, \ldots, x_n)$, where x_i for $i = 1, \ldots, n$ denotes the amount of good i. Since we can only consume positive amounts, we always have $x_i \geq 0$. A *preference relation* tells us how consumption bundles are ordered. If x and y are two consumption bundles, then we write

$$x \geq y$$

if x is deemed at least as good as y. We say that x is *preferred* to y in this case. If x is *strictly preferred* to y, which means that x is preferred to y, but y is not preferred to x, or

$$x \geq y \text{ and } y \ngeq x,$$

then we write

$$x > y.$$

If it doesn't matter which one of two consumption bundles x and y a consumer receives, then we say that the consumer is *indifferent* between x and y. This means that x is preferred to y, and y is preferred to x:

$$x \geq y \text{ and } y \geq x.$$

In this case we write

$$x \sim y.$$

When the consumer is an apartment buyer, he or she usually looks at a number of units for sale in a specific regional market. Being presented several options, the buyer is likely to prefer one apartment (equivalent to a consumption bundle) to another at some point in the process. Depending on how much the options differ and how important the individual features are to a buyer, this decision can be a rather straightforward one (if one unit is strictly preferred) or take time and/or require the consideration of additional factors (if the buyer is indifferent).

In order for the preference relation to make sense economically, we need to impose some conditions on the preferences. We say that a preference relation is *rational* if it satisfies the following two conditions.

Rational preference relations

- *Completeness*: For all consumption bundles x and y,

  at least one of $x \geq y$ and $y \geq x$ holds.

- *Transitivity*: For all consumption bundles x, y and z,

  if $x \geq y$ and $y \geq z$, then $x \geq z$.

Completeness means that we always can decide which out of two consumption bundles we prefer, and transitivity that if for some consumption bundles x, y and z we prefer x to y and y to z, then we also prefer x to z. In the next section we will see why these two conditions are important to impose.

1.2.2 Utility and utility functions

Working with a preference relation is cumbersome, and instead economists use *utility functions* in order to rank consumption bundles. A utility function U assigns the number $U(x)$ (the *utility*) to the consumption bundle x. We say that a utility function U *represents* the preference relation $\geq$ if

$$x \geq y \text{ if and only if } U(x) \geq U(y).$$

Note that $\geq$ on the left-hand side is a preference relation, while $\geq$ on the right-hand is an ordinary inequality between numbers. Hence, instead of working with the preference relation $\geq$, we use functions such as U.

It is not obvious that every preference relation can be represented by a utility function, and the mathematics used to prove the existence of a utility function and how properties of the preference relation translates into properties of the utility function are outside the scope of this text. We will only remark that *if the preference relation $\geq$ is not rational, then there does not exist any utility function representing it.* From now on we will work with utility functions instead of preferences, so we assume that every preference relation we consider is rational.

To simplify the presentation, we will assume that the economy consists of only two goods (but the models and results we present can be generalised to more goods than two). This means that a consumption bundle x is equal to $x = (x_1, x_2)$. We start by giving several examples of important utility functions.

Linear utility functions

In this case

$$U(x_1, x_2) = a_1 x_1 + a_2 x_2$$

for some constants $a_1, a_2 > 0$. As an example of a case where linear utility functions can be used, let good 1 be an office with 100 m² rental area, and good 2 an office with 50 m² rental area on the same floor as good 1. In this case it is reasonable to assume that

$$U(x_1, x_2) = x_1 + \frac{1}{2} x_2.$$

This means that when measuring the utility a space has for a corporate tenant, 100 m² of office area has the same utility as two offices with 50 m² each, and the total utility is equal to the total number of 100 m² offices plus half of the total number of 50 m² offices. In this case, the two types of offices are exchangable. Note that this is a fairly general example meant to introduce the concept of linear utility functions. To be realistic, more factors would need to be considered, such that for larger teams, two smaller areas (50 m²) do not have the same utility as one large area (100 m²). It is also reasonable to assume that the utility of additional space decreases at some point once all employees can be accommodated in an office.

Utility functions representing perfect complements

When there are bottlenecks or critical paths in a production, the limiting factor will determine the overall utility of the chosen production strategy. This can be described with the following utility function. Let

$$U(x_1, x_2) = \min(x_1, a x_2)$$

for some constant $a > 0$. Now consider the mounting of prefabricated façade elements at a construction project. In this case there are two crucial factors: The capacity of the crane (how many elements can be mounted per day?) and the storage space on site (how many elements can be stored on site at once?). The faster the crane the better, but only to the extent that elements are available for installation. Assume that a crane can mount five elements per day. With one crane the best match is to have five elements stored on site, with two cranes the best match is to have ten elements stored on site, and so on. With x_1 denoting the number of cranes and x_2 the number of prefabricated elements stored on site it is reasonable to use the utility function

$$U(x_1, x_2) = \min\left(x_1, \frac{x_2}{5}\right).$$

To undertand why this is the case, assume that we have one crane, i.e. $x_1 = 1$. The utility as a function of the number of prefabricated elements x_2 is then

$$U(1, x_2) = \begin{cases} 1/5 & \text{if } x_2 = 1 \\ 2/5 & \text{if } x_2 = 2 \\ 3/5 & \text{if } x_2 = 3 \\ 4/5 & \text{if } x_2 = 4 \\ 1 & \text{if } x_2 = 5 \\ 1 & \text{if } x_2 = 6 \\ 1 & \text{if } x_2 = 7 \\ \vdots & \vdots \end{cases}$$

Thus, with one crane we get the highest utility ($= 1$) when $x_2 \geq 5$, but when the number of prefabricated elements increases over five, the elements cannot be mounted, and the utility is not increasing.

Cobb-Douglas utility functions

Similar to the linear utility function, another example of a utility function is the Cobb-Douglas utility function. In this case

$$U(x_1, x_2) = x_1^a x_2^{1-a}$$

for a constant $0 < a < 1$. This is a utility function that does not have a clear interpretation by just studying the function, but we will see later on that it is possible to interpret the parameter a in economical terms. We will later on in this chapter see examples of the use of the Cobb-Douglas utility function.

Quasilinear utility functions

A utility function is called *quasilinear* if it is of the form

$$U(x_1, x_2) = v(x_1) + x_2$$

for some function v. This name comes from the fact that the utility function is linear in x_2, but not in x_1. Again, this is a type of utility function that, as the Cobb-Douglas utility function, is easier to give an economical interpretation when we put it in an applied context. This is done later on in this chapter.

The goal for an individual is to maximise his or her utility. As a preparation for how this is done, we will look at some general aspects of utility functions. If we fix a utility level $\overline{U}$, and consider

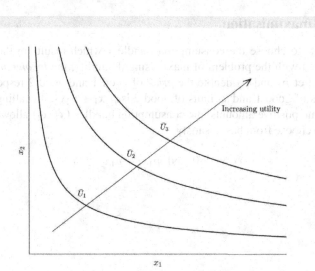

Figure 1.1: Indifferent curves and utility levels.

all consumption bundles that generate the utility $\overline{U}$, then we get an *indifference curve*. Figure 1.1 shows one example of indifference curves. Different types of utility functions will result in different types of indifference curves, but for every given utility function, the indifference curves have some common properties.

> **Properties of indifference curves**
>
> - Each consumption bundle lies on exactly one indifference curve.
>
> - Indifference curves cannot cross.
>
> - The utility of an indifference curve is higher the further away from the origin it is.

Let us look at the concept of utility in the context of residential housing. On a more detailed level, each residential apartment has its unique characteristics (size, year of construction, rooms, ceiling height, location, etc.) and amenities (kitchen, building and neighbourhood infrastructure, storage options, parking lots, etc.). The apartment buyer attributes a certain degree of usefulness to each of these characteristics which in total can be described by a utility function. Apartments that in total are of similar attractiveness to the buyer lie on the same indifference curve, while other have a higher or lower utility (i.e., *lie on a higher or lower indifference curve*). Remember that utility – and hence the attractiveness of an apartment in this example – is a subjective, individual concept: Buyer A (e.g., a doctor in a hospital) may draw a high utility from a central location and proximity to the workplace, while Buyer B (e.g., a freelancer working from home) may appreciate a large apartment with additional work rooms and a quiet neighbourhood much more.

1.2.3 Utility maximisation

A consumer wants to choose the consumption bundle x which results in the highest possible utility. When faced with the problem of maximising the utility, the *income m* of the consumer comes into play. Let p_1 and p_2 denote the *price* of good 1 and good 2 respectively. The cost of buying x_1 units of good 1 and x_2 units of good 2 is $p_1x_1 + p_2x_2$. Recalling that we are only allowed to consume positive amounts, the consumption bundles (x_1, x_2) allowed for a consumer with income m to choose from has to satisfy

$$x_1, x_2 \geq 0 \text{ and } p_1x_1 + p_1x_2 \leq m.$$

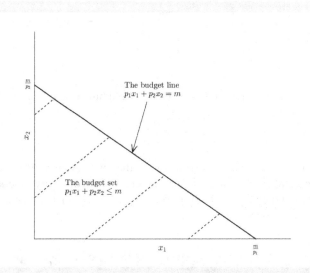

Figure 1.2: Budget set and budget line.

The allowed consumption bundles constitute the *budget set*. The straight line

$$p_1x_1 + p_2x_2 = m$$

for which both x_1 and x_2 are positive is called the *budget constraint* or the *budget line*. The budget line can be written

$$x_2 = -\frac{p_1}{p_2}x_1 + \frac{m}{p_2},$$

from which we see that the slope of the budget line is $-p_1/p_2$. In microeconomics, when defining a straight line, such as the budget line, it is practical to define it by the line's intersection with the two axes (in this case the x_1-axis and the x_2-axis). Setting $x_1 = 0$ we get the point where the straight line intersect the x_2-axis; for the budget line this results in $x_2 = m/p_2$. In the same way, setting $x_2 = 0$ results in the point where the budget line intersects the x_1-axis: $x_1 = m/p_1$. See Figure 1.2 for a graphical depiction.

Properties of the budget line

$$\text{The intersection with the } x_1\text{-axis} \;=\; \frac{m}{p_1}$$

$$\text{The intersection with the } x_2\text{-axis} \;=\; \frac{m}{p_2}$$

$$\text{The slope of the budget line} \;=\; -\frac{p_1}{p_2}.$$

In order to maximise the utility, the consumer solves the maximisation problem

$$\max_{x_1, x_2} U(x_1, x_2) \text{ subject to } p_1 x_1 + p_2 x_2 = m.$$

To solve this problem, the "neat" mathematical method is to use the Lagrange multiplier method. However, in the presented case of only two goods, we will use a simplified calculation. For more than two goods, the general result that we will derive can be extended using the Lagrange multiplier method. Returning to the maximisation problem, we start by observing that using the budget line we get

$$x_2 = \frac{m - p_1 x_1}{p_2} = -\frac{p_1}{p_2} x_1 + \frac{m}{p_2}.$$

We then insert this into the utility function, to arrive at the maximisation problem

$$\max_{x_1} U\left(x_1, -\frac{p_1}{p_2} x_1 + \frac{m}{p_2}\right).$$

This is a maximisation problem over one variable x_1. Taking the derivative[3] of this utility function with respect to x_1 and setting this equal to 0 yields

$$\frac{\partial U}{\partial x_1} + \frac{\partial U}{\partial x_2} \cdot \left(-\frac{p_1}{p_2}\right) = 0 \quad \Leftrightarrow \quad -\frac{\partial U}{\partial x_2} \cdot \frac{p_1}{p_2} = -\frac{\partial U}{\partial x_1}.$$

This equation can be written

$$-\frac{\frac{\partial U}{\partial x_1}}{\frac{\partial U}{\partial x_2}} = -\frac{p_1}{p_2}. \tag{1.1}$$

Now fix a utility level $\bar{U}$ and consider all consumption bundles (x_1, x_2) that gives this utility:

$$U(x_1, x_2) = \bar{U}.$$

Taking the derivative with respect to x_1 of this relation results in

$$\frac{\partial U}{\partial x_1} + \frac{\partial U}{\partial x_2} \cdot \frac{dx_2}{dx_1} = 0.$$

Rearranging this we get

$$\frac{dx_2}{dx_1} = -\frac{\frac{\partial U}{\partial x_1}}{\frac{\partial U}{\partial x_2}}.$$

---

[3]Here we use derivatives and partial derivatives. They are used throughout the book, and are important tools in economics. For more on derivatives and their use, see Appendix A.1.

The expression $\frac{dx_2}{dx_1}$ is the slope of an indifference curve *with the fixed utility level* $\bar{U}$. Hence, the optimality condition in Equation (1.1) states that at the optimal point the slope of the indifference curve (the left-hand side of Equation (1.1)) is equal to the slope of the budget line (the right-hand side of Equation (1.1)). The situation is depicted graphically in Figure 1.3. The circle marks the

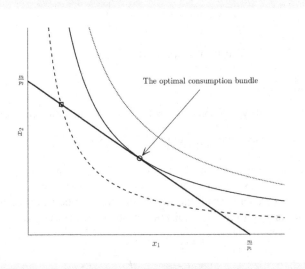

Figure 1.3: Consumption bundles.

optimal consumption bundle. The consumption bundle represented by a square is on the budget line, so it can be chosen. Note, however, that the dashed indifference curve going through this point has a lower utility than the solid indifference curve. The dotted indifference curve represents an even higher utility, but this indifference curve is not possible to reach due the limited budget of this consumer.

To understand this in a real estate context, let us revisit the example of apartment units: For the purchase decision, the apartment buyer will also take another factor into account: the total amount of money, he or she can spend on an apartment ("income"). This means that the buyer is only able to afford such units where the acquisition costs (i.e., sales price plus ancillary costs such as the notary, taxes and broker fees) are less than or equal to the amount of equity, bank loans and mortgages at his or her disposal. Given this limitation, the buyer will try to get the most attractive apartment within the budget (i.e., maximise the utility, and find the optimal consumption bundle as depicted by the circle in Figure 1.3) by balancing the various apartment features and their respective "price" factor. He or she could of course also buy a less attractive apartment (and be on the dashed indifference curve in Figure 1.3), but this would not constitute a rational choice. The above considerations are also used to evaluate residential property prices on a more general level. Here, indicators such as annuity-to-income ratio, price-to-income ratio or price-to-rent ratio provide an indication of the affordability of home ownership.[4] As mentioned earlier, utility functions are not always linear. In the next sections, we will discuss how optimal consumption choices can be determined in those cases, using the examples of Cobb-Douglas and quasilinear

[4]https://www.bundesbank.de/resource/blob/622564/eed42a97fc6d1b734b0306c581642a1d/mL/03-standard-indicators-to-evaluate-residential-property-price-data.pdf

utility functions.

Optimal consumption for a consumer with a Cobb-Douglas utility function

A consumer has a Cobb-Douglas utility function

$$U(x_1, x_2) = x_1^a x_2^{1-a},$$

where the parameter a satisfies $0 < a < 1$. Given the budget constraint

$$p_1 x_1 + p_2 x_2 = m,$$

we know that Equation (1.1) should be satisfied for the optimal consumption bundle. With a Cobb-Douglas utility function we get

$$\frac{\partial U}{\partial x_1} = a x_1^{a-1} x_2^{1-a}$$

and

$$\frac{\partial U}{\partial x_2} = (1-a) x_1^a x_2^{-a}.$$

It follows that

$$-\frac{\frac{\partial U}{\partial x_1}}{\frac{\partial U}{\partial x_2}} = -\frac{a x_1^{a-1} x_2^{1-a}}{(1-a) x_1^a x_2^{-a}} = -\frac{a}{1-a} \cdot \frac{x_2}{x_1}.$$

This is equal to $-p_1/p_2$ at the optimal consumption bundle:

$$-\frac{a}{1-a} \cdot \frac{x_2}{x_1} = -\frac{p_1}{p_2}.$$

Solving for x_2 yields

$$x_2 = \frac{1-a}{a} \cdot \frac{p_1}{p_2} x_1.$$

We now insert this in the budget constraint:

$$p_1 x_1 + p_2 \underbrace{\frac{1-a}{a} \cdot \frac{p_1}{p_2} x_1}_{=x_2} = m \quad \Leftrightarrow \quad p_1 x_1 + \left(\frac{1}{a} - 1\right) p_1 x_1 = m.$$

From this we can now solve for x_1:

$$x_1 = \frac{am}{p_1}.$$

Using the expression for x_2 we get

$$x_2 = \frac{1-a}{a} \cdot \frac{p_1}{p_2} \cdot \underbrace{\frac{am}{p_1}}_{=x_1} = \frac{(1-a)m}{p_2}.$$

Optimal consumption for a consumer with a quasilinear utility function

Let the consumer have the quasilinear utility function

$$U(x_1, x_2) = v(x_1) + x_2.$$

We further assume that the price $p_2 = 1$, leading to the budget constraint

$$p_1 x_1 + x_2 = m.$$

Since the price of x_2 units of good 2 is x_2, and the utility function consists of the sum of the utility of good 1 and the consumed amount of good 2, we can interpret good 2 as money (to be used on the consumption of other goods). With this utility function we get

$$\frac{\partial U}{\partial x_1} = v'(x_2)$$

and

$$\frac{\partial U}{\partial x_2} = 1.$$

Hence,

$$-\frac{\frac{\partial U}{\partial x_1}}{\frac{\partial U}{\partial x_2}} = -v'(x_1).$$

This should, according to Equation (1.1), be equal to $-p_1/p_2 = -p_1$ at the optimal consumption bundle, which leads to

$$v'(x_1) = p_1.$$

By solving this for x_1 we get the demand function for good 1. To be concrete, we assume that

$$v(x_1) = \sqrt{x_1}.$$

Then

$$v'(x_1) = \frac{1}{2\sqrt{x_1}},$$

and we get

$$\frac{1}{2\sqrt{x_1}} = p_1 \iff \sqrt{x_1} = \frac{1}{2p_1} \implies x_1 = \frac{1}{4p_1^2}.$$

The amount spent on good 2 is then given by the budget constraint

$$p_1 x_1 + x_2 = m \implies x_2 = m - p_1 x_1 = m - \frac{p_1}{4p_1^2} = m - \frac{1}{4p_1}.$$

Note that if $m < 1/(4p_2)$, then this amount is negative! Consumption can, however, not be negative. In a situation like this, we get what is called a *corner solution*. A solution where the individual consumes strictly positive amounts of each good is called an *interior solution*. The two cases $m \geq 1/(4p_2)$ and $m < 1/(4p_2)$ are depicted in Figure 1.4.

In the case of a quasilinear utility function, if we solve the problem of finding the maximal utility by using Equation (1.1) and the budget constraint and we end up with a negative value of x_2, then it is optimal to set

$$x_1 = \frac{m}{p_1} \text{ and } x_2 = 0.$$

In Figure 1.4 we have depicted an interior solution (the upper circle) and a corner solution (the lower circle). The squares represents the solutions to the equation $v'(x_1) = \frac{1}{2\sqrt{x_1}} = p_1$; for an interior solution this is equal to the solution, but for a corner solution we need to set $x_2 = 0$.

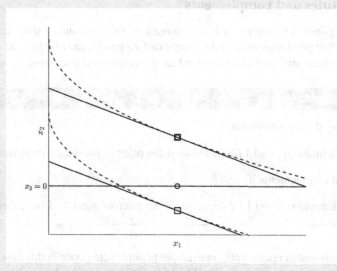

Figure 1.4: Indifference curves of a quasilinear utility function.

1.2.4 Demand

The *demand function* $D(p)$ is the amount of a good demanded by an individual or a firm if the price is p. We get an individual's demand function by looking at the solution of the individual's utility maximisation problem.

The demand function of a consumer with a Cobb-Douglas utility function

A consumer with the Cobb-Douglas utility function

$$U(x_1, x_2) = x_1^a x_2^{1-a}$$

has an optimal consumption given by

$$x_1 = \frac{am}{p_1}$$

and

$$x_2 = \frac{(1-a)m}{p_2}.$$

These are the indivdual's demand functions for good 1 and good 2 respectively. We see that a and $1 - a$ are the fraction of the income m spent on good 1 and good 2 respectively. The demanded quantities above are the demand functions for a single consumer. If there are n consumers in a market, each with an income m_j and a Cobb-Douglas utility function with parameter a_j, $j = 1, \ldots, n$, then the *market's demand function* $D(p)$ for good 1 is given by the sum of these individual demand functions:

$$D(p) = \sum_{j=1}^{n} \frac{a_j m_j}{p_1} = \frac{\sum_{j=1}^{n} a_j m_j}{p_1}.$$

In general, we get the market's demand function by adding the demand functions of the individual consumers.

1.2.5 Substitutes and complements

We say that two goods are *substitutes* if the increase in price of one of them implies that the demand for the other good increases, and we say that two goods are *complements* if the increase in price of one of them implies that the demand for the other good decreases.

Substitutes and complements

Good 1 and good 2 are substitutes if

the demand of good 1 / 2 increases if the price of good 2 / 1 increases.

The goods are complements if

the demand of good 1 / 2 decreases if the price of good 2 / 1 increases.

In the market of residential apartments, an example of substitute goods in this case are units with comparable features, for instance in one building block. The apartments may have similar sizes, were built in the same year and do not differ much in the proximity to neighbourhood amenities such as supermarkets, parks or schools. For the demand this implies that if one apartment gets more expensive, the demand for a comparable apartment will increase. Complementary goods on the other hand are for instance apartments and garages. Assuming a garage is usually bought together with an apartment nearby, the increase in apartment prices, and hence reduced overall transaction activities, are likely to lead to a decreasing demand for garages as well.

1.3 Producers

We now move on to study the production of the goods the consumers buy. Here we only consider firms that produce one good. The main questions for a producer are the following:

  1) How *much* should be produced?

  2) *How* should the desired quantity be produced?

If a firm produces the quantity q, then the *profit* π of the firm is given by

$$\pi(q) = p(\cdots)q - C(q),$$

where p is the price of the produced good, $p(\cdots)q$ is the *revenue* and $C(q)$ is the *cost* of the firm to produce the quantity q. The notation $p(\cdots)$ symbolises that the price can depend on several variables. What the price function looks like is dependent on the market form, and we will come back to this later on. For two firms in the same market and producing the same good, what distinguishes them is their *cost function* C. To answer question 1) above, the firm should choose the quantity q such that the profit $\pi(q)$ is maximised. But in order to know how much it should produce, it must know the cost of producing q units. And the cost depends on how the good is produced, hence it is determined by the answer to question 2). For this reason we start with studying the best way for a firm to produce the quantity q.

But before we do this, let us look at examples from real estate. Producers in real estate can be for instance a real estate developer for residential apartments. In general terms, the developer makes a profit by selling a certain number of units (q) at some price (p), so that the revenue is higher than the cost of land acquisition, building design and construction for the project ($C(q)$). Producers can also appear in a more abstract way in the context of real estate management services. For instance, one can think of the asset or portfolio managers as "producers". Just like the project developer or construction company described above, they also use a toolkit of technologies and processes to turn capital and human work into value-creating services for clients. This can for instance be software, databases or office equipment needed to deliver the performance in the most cost-efficient manner.

1.3.1 Costs

A firm uses *production factors* to produce goods. In order to understand both how and why the cost function differs between different firms, we need to understand the mechanism that creates output (quantity) from inputs (production factors). The way the production factors are transformed into quantity is called the firm's *technology*. We take a simple route and assume the existence of a function determining how much output is produced given the level of inputs:

$$q = f(L, K).$$

Here f is the *production function*, L the amount of *labour* and K is the amount of *capital* used by the firm. Hence, the production function explicitly describes how the production factors are transformed into the quantity produced. In order to use labour and capital, the firm has to pay the employed the wage w and the bank the interest rate r. The cost function is defined as the lowest cost at which the quantity q can be produced:

$$C(q) = \min_{L,K} (wL + rK) \text{ subject to } f(L, K) = q.$$

When realising a project (the "production"), the developer can choose from a range of delivery concepts and construction methods (the "technology"). Any of them will require a certain amount of capital and labour. However, on a more detailed level, the approaches differ: Traditional projects are structured in a rather sequential manner, with separate design, planning and construction teams (called "design-bid-build" or "design-build"). These projects are realised predominantly through on-site construction. More recently, the concept of integrated project delivery (i.e., involvement of all parties throughout design, fabrication and construction) in combination with industrialised construction has driven a shift towards model-based off-site prefabrication. Last, but not least, there is also the possibility of using robots on site to automate works like drilling or painting, and increase construction speed and safety. Note that all these concepts come with very different implications for the capital investment and human resources. It is the task of the project team to determine the one most suitable for the given site, financing (e.g., interest rates) and labour market (e.g., wage levels) constraints to deliver the project as cost-efficiently as possible.

We distinguish between the *short run* and the *long run*. In the short run it is not possible to change all production factors, while this is possible in the long run. Typically it is assumed that the amount of capital can only be changed in the long run, while the amount of labour can be changed both in the short and the long run. The reason for these assumptions is that it is in general easy to hire people when this is needed, while building new factories, i.e. investing in capital, takes much longer time. As with a fixed utility level, we use a bar above a variable to denote that the variable is fixed. Using this notation we can write the production function in the short run as

$$q = f(L, \overline{K}).$$

In this case, the cost function is given by

$$C(q) = \min_L \left(wL + r\overline{K} \right) \text{ subject to } f(L, \overline{K}) = q.$$

Letting $g(L)$ denote the inverse function of $f(L, \overline{K})$ for the fixed level of capital $\overline{K}$, we see that there is only one level of labour that satisfies the constraint

$$f(L, \overline{K}) = q,$$

namely

$$L = g(q).$$

Replacing L with $g(q)$ in $wL + r\overline{K}$ results in

$$C(q) = wg(q) + r\overline{K},$$

and this is the short-run cost function. The function $wg(q)$ is the *variable cost*, and the constant $r\overline{K}$ is the *fixed cost*.

Example 1.3.1 The production function for a firm is given by

$$q = f(L, K) = \sqrt{LK}.$$

In the short run, the capital level is fixed at $\overline{K}$. Hence, in the short run the production function for the firm is given by

$$q = \sqrt{L\overline{K}} = \sqrt{\overline{K}} \cdot \sqrt{L}.$$

Solving for L yields $L = q^2/\overline{K}$. It follows that the cost of the firm for producing q units is

$$C(q) = wL + r\overline{K} = w \cdot \frac{q^2}{\overline{K}} + r\overline{K} = \frac{w}{\overline{K}} \cdot q^2 + r\overline{K}.$$

To calculate the long-run cost function is more complicated, and we will not pursue this. Instead we introduce some important concepts regarding the cost function.

Components of cost functions

The following functions can be derived from the cost function.

- The *fixed cost* $F = C(0)$.

- The *variable cost* $VC(q) = C(q) - F$.

- The *average cost* $AC(q) = C(q)/q$.

- The *marginal cost* $MC(q) = C'(q)$.

Example 1.3.2 Returning to Example 1.3.1, we had a cost function given by

$$C(q) = \frac{w}{\overline{K}} \cdot q^2 + r\overline{K}.$$

In this case we have:

- The fixed cost $F = C(0) = r\overline{K}$.

- The variable cost $VC(q) = C(q) - F = \frac{w}{\overline{K}} \cdot q^2$.

- The average cost $AC(q) = C(q)/q = \frac{w}{\overline{K}} \cdot q + r\overline{K} \cdot \frac{1}{q}$.

- The marginal cost $MC(q) = C'(q) = \frac{2w}{\overline{K}} \cdot q$.

We end this section with the following fact: If the marginal cost is constant, then the cost function is of the form

$$C(q) = cq + F,$$

where c is the constant marginal cost and F is the fixed cost. Typically, in the short run the fixed cost $F > 0$, and in the long run the fixed cost $F = 0$.

1.3.2 Profit

Now that we know how to calculate production costs, we assess the firm's profit function. From a microeconomic point of view, a company will want to maximise its profit by choosing the optimal quantity of goods or services to produce. In mathematical terms, this means addressing the problem

$$\max_q \pi(q) = \max_q \left(pq - C(q)\right)$$

over $q \geq 0$ by first setting the derivative of $\pi(q)$ to zero, and then solving the equation

$$\pi'(q) = 0.$$

Examples of the profit function and the condition $\pi'(q) = 0$ are shown in Figure 1.5. The profit calculation in the example of residential developers follows the same procedure as described above. To find the optimal quantity to produce, the respective company will consider the production costs for each unit and in parallel analyse the market situation in terms of pricing and competition. The price will depend on the market structure the company operates in (see Section 1.3.1), i.e., whether they are the only actor in a certain market or face competition from a few or many other developers with similar apartments on offer.

Finding the quantity that maximises π can also be a way of find the quantity that minimises the loss; see Figure 1.6. If the maximum profit is negative, it might seem natural to stop the production. Due to fixed costs, this, however, need not be the case. See Exercise 1.3, where you are asked to do the analysis. Finally, we note that the profit can be written

$$\pi(q) = pq - C(q) = q\left(p - \frac{C(q)}{q}\right) = q(p - AC(q)).$$

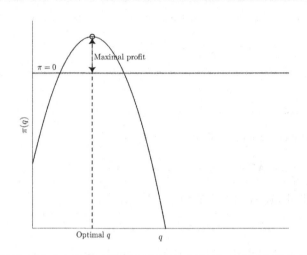

Figure 1.5: Optimal quantity and maximised profit.

This means that the relation between the price p and the average cost $AC(q)$ at the chosen level q of production determines the sign of the firm's profit. In order to explicitly calculate the profit function, we need to understand how the price p at which the product is sold is determined, and this is the topic of the next section.

1.4 Markets

The consumers and the produces meet in a *market*. There any many types of different market structures, and the prevailing type of market is crucial when the firm calculates the quantity it should produce. In real estate, the "markets" relevant for a specific actor can be defined in various ways. When determining a production strategy, the perspective will most likely consider the asset class first, i.e., the type of property offered or demanded by the consumers: offices, apartments, warehouses, hotels, etc. Since real estate is very location-specific though and also heterogeneous in itself (unlike, e.g., shoes), markets could also be thought of from a locational perspective (e.g., only the German market or only the Frankfurt market), and only in a second step look at a specific asset class. This could apply for instance to an investment company looking to acquire properties in a certain country to diversify the portfolio risks.

The aforementioned, special characteristics of real estate markets are important to keep in mind when discussing microeconomics examples based on real assets (e.g., apartments, office buildings, hotels). Unlike consumer goods of which thousands can be produced in an identical way, properties are very heterogeneous due to their immobile nature. In addition, property markets are rather intransparent, especially in the case of commercial real estate where transaction prices and deals are not always disclosed. In contrast to stocks or bonds, real assets are also much less fungible with high transaction costs and often a time span of several months between the first property visit and the deal closing. Given the large transaction volumes and management complexity, entry barriers to professional real estate investment are comparatively high. Last but

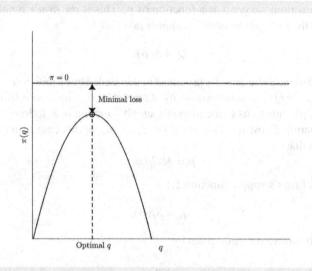

Figure 1.6: Optimal quantity and minimised loss.

not least, due to long leases and construction periods, time lags of several years until the supply adjusts to the demand are common. For instance, a recession period in the overall economy will only hit the real estate market with a severe delay. Likewise, it takes the real estate market longer to recover from a recession period than the overall economy. Depending on the context of the examples in this book, we sometimes generalise for the sake of simplicity.

1.4.1 Competitive markets

In a *competitive market*, also known as a *perfectly competitive market*, the firms are *price takers*, i.e. they cannot influence the price of the good they are selling. Real estate developers in a competitive market will have to sell their apartments at the price set by the market, irrespective of their internal costs. If the price set by the developer is higher than the market price, potential buyers will simply switch to another developer. An individual market stakeholder will not have enough influence to change the price. The only lever the developer has for profit optimisation is hence the cost function of the apartment production, e.g., by choosing a different construction method or negotiating better financing terms for the project.

If the market form is a competitive market, then the price p of the good the firm produces is set through an equilibrium on the market level, and the firm takes this p as given, i.e. it is a constant. This means that for a firm operating on a competitive market the profit function is

$$\pi(q) = pq - C(q),$$

and the profit maximising condition is

$$\pi'(q) = p - C'(q) = 0.$$

The last equation can be written

$$p = MC(q).$$

By inverting this function, we get q as a function of p. This is *the firm's supply function*. If we sum over all firms, then we get *the market's supply function S*:

$$Q = S(p).$$

Note that we use q to denote the quantity produced or demanded by an individual firm or consumer, respectively, and we use Q to denote the quantity at market level. The detailed procedure of getting from individual supply functions to the market's supply function is as follows. The market has n firms, each with marginal cost function MC_i, $i = 1, \ldots, n$. In this case firm i wants to produce the amount q_i such that

$$p = MC_i(q_i).$$

Inverting this gives firm i's supply function S_i:

$$q_i = S_i(p).$$

The market's supply function is now given by

$$Q = \sum_{i=1}^{n} q_i = \sum_{i=1}^{n} S_i(p) = S(p).$$

Market equilibrium

In a competitive market, the market price p is set by demanding that the market is in *equilibrium*. The *equilibrium condition* is that market demand equals market supply:

$$D(p) = S(p).$$

Hence, the market price p is such that market demand is equal to market supply.

Example 1.4.1 Assume that the market's demand function for small apartments in a minor European city is

$$D(p) = 100 - 2p,$$

and that the corresponding supply function is given by

$$S(p) = 20 + 2p.$$

Here, the price is in €1,000. The equilibrium price is found by solving

$$D(p) = S(p)$$

(the equilibrium condition). In this case we get

$$100 - 2p = 20 + 2p \quad \Leftrightarrow \quad 4p = 80 \quad \Rightarrow \quad p = 20,$$

so the market price of a small apartment in this city is €20,000. The quantity produced at this price can be found either by inserting this price into the demand function

$$Q = D(20) = 100 - 2 \cdot 20 = 60,$$

or by using the supply function

$$Q = S(20) = 20 + 2 \cdot 20 = 60.$$

This means that in equilibrium, there will be 60 apartments of this size sold, and the price of each apartment is €20,000.

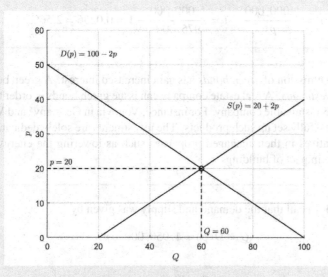

Figure 1.7: Market equilibrium.

Market equilibria also prevail on financial markets. A *bond* is a financial instrument that gives the owner fixed payouts at fixed dates. Bonds are issued by both governments and firms in order to finance their activities. Associated with a bond is an *interest rate*, also known as the bond's *yield*. This interest rate is determined in equilibrium from the demand and supply of the bond.

Example 1.4.2 Assume that the demand for bonds with one payment of €1,000,000 in 1 year's time, is given by
$$Q = D(p) = 1,950,000 - p,$$
and the supply is given by
$$Q = S(p) = p.$$
The price of this bond in a competitive equilibrium is given by the price p satisfying
$$D(p) = S(p),$$
which in this case is

$$1,950,000 - p = p \iff 2p = 1,950,000 \implies p = €975,000.$$

The interest rate r of this bond is defined by

$$p = \frac{1,000,000}{1+r},$$

where p is the price of the bond. Hence, given the price in equilibrium, we can determine the equilibrium interest rate:

$$r = \frac{1,000,000}{p} - 1 = \frac{1,000,000}{975,000} - 1 = 0.0256 = 2.56\%.$$

In recent years, the emission of *green bonds* has gain increased interest. A green bond is a way of financing *green investments*. A real estate company can issue green bonds in order to finance their transition to a more sustainable company. For instance, Vonovia in Germany[5] and Vasakronan[6] in Sweden have successfully set up such products. The investments are solely dedicated to financing sustainability initiatives in their managed properties such as lowering the energy consumption and overall climate impact of buildings.

Example 1.4.3 Recall that the demand and supply was given by

$$Q = D(p) = 1,950,000 - p,$$

and

$$Q = S(p) = p$$

respectively, which resulted in an equilibrium price of $p = €975,000$ and an equilibrium rate of $r = 2.56\%$. Now consider a green bond giving the investor €1,000,000 in one year's time. For this green version of the bond, the demand function is given by

$$D_g(p) = 1,980,000 - p,$$

while we assume that the supply function is the same as for the ordinary bond:

$$S_g(p) = p.$$

In this case the equilibrium condition

$$D_g(p) = S_g(p)$$

results in the equilibrium price

$$1,980,000 - p = p \quad \Leftrightarrow \quad 2p = 1,980,000 \quad \Rightarrow \quad p = €990,000.$$

The interest rate in equilibrium is given by

$$r = \frac{1,000,000}{990,000} - 1 = 0.0101 = 1.01\%.$$

[5]https://presse.vonovia.de/en/aktuelles/220322-vonovia-emittiert-social-bonds-in-hoehe-von-2-5-mrd-euro
[6]https://vasakronan.se/en/about-vasakronan/financial-information/financing/bonds/

In this example, the price of a green bond is higher than for an equivalent ordinary bond, resulting in a lower interest rate in equilibrium. Since this interest rate can be thought of as the interest rate at which an issuer (such as a government or a firm) can borrow money, this in turn means that it will be cheaper to finance a green investment than an ordinary one. But, on the other hand, why would an investor accept this lower interest rate?

Presently, the real estate market is seeing that in anticipation of regulatory changes (as the EU taxonomy for sustainability activities) property owners push for initiatives such as energy efficiency improvements or mobility concepts. To finance this, green bonds are a suitable instrument, because it is a win-win situation: The property owner gets money for investments in the building, which increase the lettability and decrease their exposure to climate risks. Therefore, the property value and rental income increases. In consequence, the investors can receive attractive returns which further drives the investment in green bonds rather than brown equivalents. They also can report sustainable investments on their own and/or classify their products as sustainable (e.g., if the bond purchases are part of the investment activities in a multi-asset portfolio). Ordinary bonds could be used to finance sustainable investments as well, but green bonds have the specific and secured purpose to do so, i.e., it is more transparent and targeted for the investors. However, the attractiveness of green bonds has raised the issue of so-called greenwashing, meaning that companies may attempt to stretch the limits in order to get a product such as a bond being classified as green.

Elasticities

In order to measure how the demand and supply is influenced by a change in price, we use the *price elasticity of demand*

$$\varepsilon = \frac{p}{D(p)} \cdot \frac{dD(p)}{dp},$$

and the *price elasticity of supply*

$$\eta = \frac{p}{S(p)} \cdot \frac{dS(p)}{dp}.$$

Since we expect the demand function to be downward sloping, and the supply function to be upward sloping, we see that $\varepsilon \leq 0$ and $\eta \geq 0$.

Replacing the derivative with a ratio of changes we get

$$\varepsilon \approx \frac{p}{D(p)} \cdot \frac{\Delta D(p)}{\Delta p} \quad \Leftrightarrow \quad \frac{\Delta D(p)}{D(p)} \approx \varepsilon \frac{\Delta p}{p}$$

and

$$\eta \approx \frac{p}{S(p)} \cdot \frac{\Delta S(p)}{\Delta p} \quad \Leftrightarrow \quad \frac{\Delta S(p)}{S(p)} \approx \eta \frac{\Delta p}{p}$$

respectively. Hence, we see that these quantities measure how much a relative change in the price $\Delta p / p$ translates into the relative change $\Delta D(p)/D(p)$ in demand and relative change $\Delta S(p)/S(p)$ in supply respectively.

In real estate and urban economics it is common as a first approximation to assume that the supply function of housing is perfectly inelastic as in Figure 1.8. Here, the supply function S, the initial

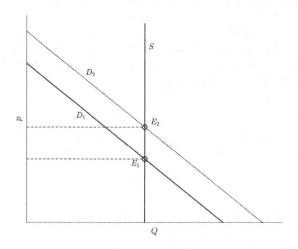

Figure 1.8: Short-term price elasticity of housing supply.

demand function D_1 and initial equilibrium E_1 and finally the new demand funtion D_2 and the new equilibrium E_2 are depicted. When the demand functions shifts from the original demand function D_1 to, say, D_2, then the only effect will be on the new equilibrium price, while the quantity at equilibrium will be the same. In practice, this is a short-term view: If the demand for housing in a certain area increases, the prices will go up, but no additional units will be available immediately. It is also applicable to other asset classes, e.g., offices. Especially in commercial real estate, this is because of the time lag in the reaction of real estate markets to general market cycles and trends in the broader economy. At the beginning of a macroeconomic growth or recession period and hence a shift in demand for office spaces driven by corporate expansion strategies, it takes time for the real estate supply to catch up. Again, in the short run only the prices react (if at all, depending on the average lease periods and contractual flexibility), not the physical supply.

In the longer run, it is more realistic to assume that the supply function is not perfectly inelastic, but that it is highly inealastic. An example of this is shown in Figure 1.9. It usually takes a real estate market several years to adjust the supply to economic trends due to the long lead time until a project's planning and construction is completed. In contrast, the price elasticity of demand is higher in the case of real estate. In markets with high price elasticity, buyers are more sensitive to price changes. If an apartment is being offered at a slightly higher price, the demand will be reduced significantly. In larger cities with challenging housing markets, the demand is often less elastic and will remain at a similar level – even if the prices increase, people will still buy or rent apartments due to a general shortage in housing.

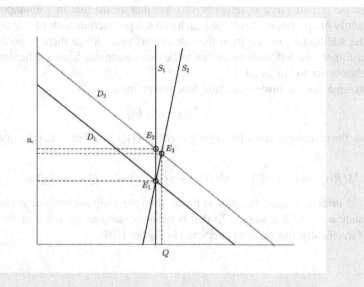

Figure 1.9: Short- and long-term price elasticity of housing supply.

The supply function is S_2, the initial demand function D_1 and initial equilibrium E_1, the new demand funtion D_2 and the new equilibrium E_3. As a reference, the supply function S_1 and the equilibrium E_2 from Figure 1.8 is also present.

1.4.2 Monopolies

When there is only one producer of a good, the market form is called a *monopoly*. In this case, the whole quantity supplied to the market is from one firm, so in this case the firm that is the monopolist produces the market quantity Q. In order to choose the optimal quantity, the firm should choose the quantity that maximises

$$\pi(Q) = p(Q)Q - C(Q).$$

Here $p(Q)$ is the *inverse demand function*, defined as the inverse D^{-1} of the market's demand function:

$$Q = D(p) \quad \Rightarrow \quad p = D^{-1}(Q).$$

Returning to the monopolist's profit maximisation problem, we get

$$\pi'(Q) = p'(Q)Q + p(Q) - C'(Q).$$

The expression

$$MR(Q) = p'(Q)Q + p(Q)$$

is the *marginal revenue*, and the optimality condition $\pi'(Q) = 0$ can be written

$$MR(Q) - MC(Q) = 0,$$

or

$$MR(Q) = MC(Q).$$

In the example of real estate developers, this formula means that in a monopoly the actor will set the quantity of apartments developed such that the production costs of one additional unit are equal to the additional revenue from the sale of this unit. Since there is no competitor in the market, customers are left with no choice to buy an apartment from a different developer, they can only choose not to buy at all.

Now assume that the inverse demand function is linear:

$$p(Q) = a - bQ.$$

In this case, the revenue is given by $p(Q)Q = (a - bQ)Q$. It follows that the marginal revenue is given by

$$MR(Q) = \big(p(Q)Q\big)' = p'(Q)Q + p(Q) = (-b) \cdot Q + a - bQ = a - 2bQ.$$

Hence, if the inverse demand function is linear, then the marginal revenue is also linear with the same constant a but with a slope $-2b$ that is twice as steep as the slope of the inverse demand function. Graphically, this results is depicted in Figure 1.10

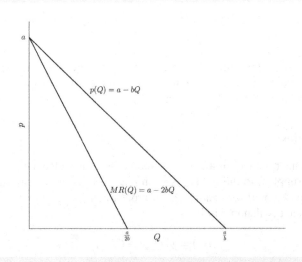

Figure 1.10: Marginal revenue of linear inverse demand functions.

Example 1.4.4 The inverse demand function for residential apartments is given by

$$p(Q) = 10 - Q,$$

and the cost function of firms building residential apartments is, in hundred millions of euros, $C(q) = 4q$. If there exists one firm which builds residential apartments, then the market is a monopoly. In this case the optimal quantity Q satisfies

$$MR(Q) = MC(Q).$$

In this example

$$MR(Q) = 10 - 2Q \text{ and } MC(Q) = 4,$$

and we get

$$10 - 2Q = 4 \iff 6 = 2Q \implies Q = 3.$$

This is the quantity that the monopolist wants to produce. The price the monopolist sets is

$$p = 10 - 3 = 7$$

and the profit is

$$\pi = 7 \cdot 3 - 4 \cdot 3 = 9.$$

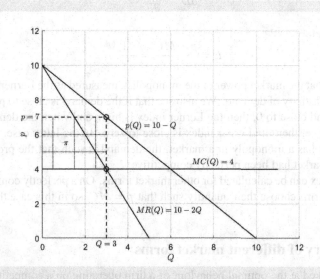

Figure 1.11: Maximisation of monopolistic profit.

The fact that the monopolist can charge a price higher than the marginal cost, and hence make a strictly positive profit in equilibrium (as opposed the case of a competitive market) is referred to as the monopolist's *market power*. In order to measure the market power of a monopolist, we can use the *Lerner index L*. This index is defined as the price minus the marginal cost, divided by the price:

$$L = \frac{p - MC}{p}.$$

We know from above, that the monopolist's optimality condition $\pi'(Q) = 0$ is equivalent to

$$p'(Q)Q + p(Q) - C'(Q) = 0 \quad \Leftrightarrow \quad p(Q) - C'(Q) = -p'(Q)Q,$$

or, since $C' = MC$,

$$\frac{p - MC}{p} = -\frac{dp}{dQ} \cdot Qp.$$

But since $Q = D(p)$ in this case, we see that

$$\frac{dp}{dQ} \cdot \frac{Q}{p} = \frac{dp}{dD} \cdot \frac{D}{p} = \frac{1}{\frac{dD}{dp} \cdot \frac{p}{D}} = \frac{1}{\varepsilon},$$

where ε is the price elasticity of demand and we have used the fact that

$$\frac{dp}{dD} = \frac{1}{\frac{dD}{dp}}.$$

Summarising we get

$$L = \frac{p - MC}{p} = -\frac{1}{\varepsilon}.$$

The conclusion is that the market power of the monopolist, measured as the Lerner index, depends only on the price elasticity of demand. We also see that if the demand is close to perfectly elastic, i.e. ε is negative and close to 0, then the Lerner index is high, and when the demand is close to inelastic, i.e. $\varepsilon \approx -\infty$, then the Lerner index is close to zero. In the latter case, this means that even though a firm has a monopoly in a market, the demand is such that the profit is not much larger than if the market had been perfectly competitive.

The Lerner index can be calculated for other market forms. On a perfectly competitive market we know that the firms choose their quantity such that $p = MC$, so in this case the Lerner index is $L = 0$.

1.4.3 Summary of different market forms

So far we have looked at the optimal behaviour of a firm operating on a competitive market and being a monopolist. In Chapter 3 we will study what happens if the market form is an *oligopoly*, which is a market form consisting of a "few" number of firms producing different goods which in general are substitutes, but need not be identical.

> **Overview: Market forms**
>
> - *A competitive market:* The price is set by the market, and the firm is a price-taker. The price is a constant p.
>
> - *A monopoly:* The price is set uniquely by the firm. The price is a function $p(Q)$ of the quantity supplied to the market.
>
> - *An oligopoly:* The market consists of a finite number $n \geq 2$ of firms. If the firms are producing the same good, then the price is a function $p(q_1 + q_2 + \ldots + q_n)$ of the sum of the quantity produced by each firm.
>
> - *The general case:* The market consists of a finite number $n \geq 2$ of firms not necessarily producing the same good. The price of the good produced by firm k, for $k = 1, \ldots, n$, is given by a function $p_k(q_1, q_2, \ldots, q_n)$ of the quantity produced by each firm.

1.5   Welfare

In an attempt to ensure the economic well-being of individuals and the society as a whole, the concept of welfare is introduced. By measuring welfare, we want to understand, how equilibria and regulations affect the economic surplus of consumers, producers and the state. This allows to compare different scenarios from a holistic perspective and discuss whether they benefit all or only a few actors. For residential apartments, the notion of the consumers' welfare as well as the producers', and the overall welfare is at the core of many political and societal debates: How can communities be provided with affordable housing in a way that is still financially viable for real estate developers? The developers have to generate a profit by producing housing units at a price higher than the marginal construction costs, while the apartment buyers need to be able to afford adequate housing without spending their entire income on an apartment.

1.5.1   Welfare for consumers and producers

In order to measure the welfare of a consumer we use the *consumer's surplus* (*CS*). This is the area between the consumer's demand function and the market price for all quantities from 0 up to the quantity demanded; see the graph in Figure 1.12. To measure the welfare of firms we use the *producer's surplus* (*PS*). This is defined as the area between the market price and the firm's marginal cost up to the produced quantity; see Figure 1.13. There is a clear economic interpretation of the producer's surplus. By using the definition of the producer's surplus we get

$$
\begin{aligned}
PS &= \int_0^q (p - MC(x))dx \\
&= pq - (C(q) - C(0)) \\
&= pq - C(q) + C(0) \\
&= \pi(q) + F.
\end{aligned}
$$

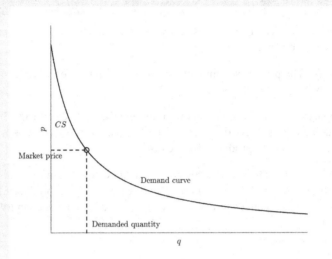

Figure 1.12: Consumer's surplus.

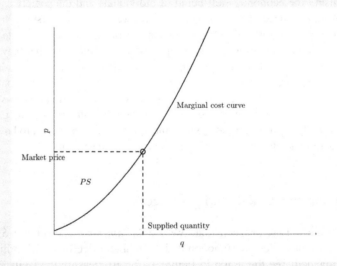

Figure 1.13: Producer's surplus.

Hence, choosing the quantity q that maximises the producer's surplus is the same as choosing the quantity that maximises the profit of the firm. Why do we use the consumer's surplus to measure the welfare of an individual? This is a harder question to answer, but if the utility function of an individual is quasilinear (see Section 1.2.2 above for the definition), then we can interpret the consumer's surplus as the amount an individual needs to be compensated for if the price of a good increases. Alternatively, we can interpret it as the amount an individual is willing to give up to avoid the increase in price. But note that these properties are only guaranteed to hold if the utility function is quasilinear.

1.5.2 Welfare on market level

When we use the market's demand function for a good, we get the *consumers' surplus* which we still denote CS, and this is the quantity that represents the total welfare of the consumers. In the same way, we use the market supply function in order to determine the *producers' supply*, again denoted PS, as the measure of the welfare of firms on an aggregate level. Finally, we need to consider welfare effects for the government. The government can dispose of several tools to affect welfare, for instance taxes, subsidies, tariffs and trade barriers. In this book, we will, however, only consider one possible welfare effect regarding the government, namely in the case the government imposes a tax with total value T. This will give the government an income of T, and using all these parts we define the total welfare W as

$$W = CS + PS + T.$$

1.5.3 Pareto efficiency

An allocation of goods is *Pareto efficient* (or *Pareto optimal*) if every reallocation of the allocation makes at least one of the participants in the allocation (e.g., individuals or firms) less well off. If an allocation is Pareto efficient, then there is no way of changing it without at least one individual or firm becoming worse off. There is a close connection between Pareto-efficient allocations and the competitive market equilibrium. In many economic models, the following two claims are true.

Fundamental theorems of welfare economics

The First Theorem of Welfare Economics
The competitive equilibrium is Pareto efficient.

The Second Theorem of Welfare Economics
Any Pareto-efficient allocation can be achieved by competition.

If we end up in an equilibrium which is not equal to the competive equilibrium, then there will be a loss in welfare. This is known as a *deadweight loss* (DWL). The loss in welfare can arise due to the fact that the market is a monopoly or due to the fact that the cost function of the society, known as the *social cost function* is not equal to the cost function of the firm.

Finally, it should be noted that in essentially every case of an investment by some kind of governmental organisation, such as building a new road, a bridge or an airport, there will never be a *Pareto improvement*, i.e. a new allocation of resources that makes no one worse off. In these cases the *Kaldor-Hicks criterion* is more suitable: If the *total* welfare increases if an investment is done, then the investment should be done. In order to fully or partially compensate the ones who became worse off, the increase in welfare can then be used by letting the welfare be redistributed.

1.6 Literature notes

A more comprehensive treatment of the micronomics presented here can be found in Perloff [43] or Varian [53]. More advanced texts include Gravelle & Rees [17], Mas-Colell, Whinston & Green [35] and Varian [52].

1.7 Exercises

Exercise 1.1 An inexperienced apartment buyer only looks at the proximity to the city centre (x_1) and the proximity to the park areas (x_2) to make his investment decision. The proximity is measured such that the closer an apartment is to either of the two factors, the higher is the value of x_1 and x_2 respectively. We model this situation by the utility function

$$U(x_1, x_2) = x_1 + x_2.$$

a) Draw this apartment buyer's indifference curves fo utility levels $\overline{U} = 1$, $\overline{U} = 3$ and $\overline{U} = 5$.

b) If the price of apartments is such that the proximity to park areas is priced at twice the price of the proximity to the city centre, i.e. $p_2 = 2p_1$, then how will the apartment buyer choose an apartment?

Exercise 1.2 A building design requires the use of steel and concrete as main components of the superstructure. The construction company can use a certain amount of raw material to realise the design – if one resource is limited, the project cannot be scaled. The amount of steel, x_1, and the amount of concrete, x_2, are both measured in tons.

a) Using the utility function
$$U(x_1, x_2) = \min(x_1, x_2),$$

draw the indifference curves for this utility function at the utility levels $\overline{U} = 1$, $\overline{U} = 2$ and $\overline{U} = 3$.

b) The price of steel is €150 per ton, and the price of concrete is €50 per ton. Draw the budget line if the construction company has a budget of $m =$ €10,000.

c) Derive geometrically the optimal amounts of steel and concrete when the prices are as in b).

d) Derive the demand function of steel.

Exercise 1.3 In a new residential district, several developers are realising apartments of a certain standard. Assuming perfect competition, the price for an apartment is set at p. One developer has the cost function
$$C(q) = 10{,}000q^2 + 10{,}000{,}000.$$

Determine the optimal quantity of apartments to build for this developer in the following cases:

a) $p =$ €1,800,000.

b) $p = €600,000$.

Exercise 1.4 The overall market demand for single family houses in a small town is

$$Q = D(p) = 100,000 - p,$$

while the market supply function is given by

$$Q = S(p) = 2p - 20,000.$$

a) In an equilibrium, which quantity is produced at what price?

b) How large is the consumers' and producers' surplus respectively?

c) Which quantity is produced at equilibrium, and what is the equilibrium price if the demand instead is given by

$$Q = D(p) = \frac{120,000}{p},$$

and

$$Q = S(p) = 30,000p$$

repectively?

Exercise 1.5 The demand for bonds with one payment of €1,000,000 in 1 year's time, is given by

$$Q = D(p) = 1,950,000 - p,$$

and the supply is given by

$$Q = S(p) = p.$$

a) How large is the price of this bond in equilibrium?

The interest rate r of this bond is defined by

$$p = \frac{1,000,000}{1 + r},$$

where p is the price of the bond from a).

b) How large is the interest rate of this bond in equilibrium?

Exercise 1.6 In a competitive market with 12 market actors, the demand for large one-family houses is described by

$$D(p) = 50,000 - 1,900p,$$

where p is the price in €100,000, and the cost for each market actor is given by the cost function

$$C(q) = 0.01q^2.$$

What will the price of a small one-family house be?

Exercise 1.7 A real estate investor plans to bring a new hotel concept to market. Since this is a unique concept, the investor is a monopolist. Following a standardised concept, each hotel is expected to cost about €2m. Therefore, we assume the cost function

$$C(Q) = 2Q,$$

where the cost is in million of euros. Initial market research among potential buyers has yielded an inverse demand function of

$$p(Q) = 10 - 2Q;$$

again, the price is in million of euros.

a) How many hotels does the real estate investor build, and how large is the profit?

Now assume that fixed costs $F > 0$ are considered in the cost function to account for overhead costs and production facilities. The resulting cost function hence is

$$C(Q) = 2Q + F.$$

b) How many hotels does the real estate investor build, and how large is the profit in this case?

Exercise 1.8 The demand for medium-sized apartments is given by

$$Q = D(p) = 10,000 - 2p$$

(here Q is the number of apartments, and p is the monthly rent for an apartment measured in euros), and the supply of medium-sized apartments is given by

$$Q = S(p) = 6p.$$

a) At what monthly rent is the demand of medium-sized apartments equal to zero?

b) How many apartments are built, and what is the monthly rent if the market is a competitive market?

In some countries there exists *rent regulation*, regulating the maximal rent a landlord is allowed to charge to a tenant. The reason for doing this is to make it possible for families with lower incomes to rent apartments. The drawback is a reduced construction of new apartments and in consequence also a welfare loss.

c) If the government set the maximum rent allowed to charge for a medium-sized apartment to €1,000 per month, how many medium-sized apartments are buildt?

d) How large is the welfare loss if the rent regulation is set to €1,000?

Chapter 2

Game theory

In this chapter, the fundamentals of game theory are presented. Equilibria and response strategies are discussed in various forms of both static and dynamic games. Like microeconomic concepts, game theory is naturally present in business situations and helps to reflect on strategic decision-making such as in lease negotiations or large-scale industry transformations.

2.1 Introduction

The foundations of information economics are, generally speaking, microeconomics and game theory. We looked at the basics of microeconomics in the previous chapter, and in this we are going to introduce the reader to game theory. The following is a list of the parts in the games that we are going to study.

- *Players*: The ones playing the game. They could e.g. be individuals, firms or countries. In a real estate context, players are for instance leasing managers, real estate investment companies or the industry as a whole who interact with other stakeholders inside and outside their field.

- *Actions*: The possible choices the players can do. A leasing manager for example can take different actions: make a rental offer or adjust it (e.g., the rent, the space, the fit-out quality, etc.), enter into negotiations with a potential tenant or not, advertise a space, etc.

- *Strategies*: A set of actions. The actions taken and their respective order – often in response to their counterpart's (anticipated) action – characterise the strategy of the players in the example of leasing: Will the manager market a vacant property aggressively, will they wait for economic trends to drive rental levels, will they make compromises or push for their maximal target?

- *Payoffs*: The payout to each player at the end of the game. As a result of the strategy chosen by a leasing manager, the payoff could be a signed lease contract and hence increased rental income, or the end of negotiations without any agreement. Note that between the optimal outcome (agreement with target conditions) and the least optimal outcome (no agreement) there is a range of potential outcomes depending on how much the parties are willing to compromise.

- *Rules*: Determine how the games is played, including the set of actions, strategies and how large the payoff to each player is. The payoff and the set of actions taken are defined by internal and external rules the players are subject to. In the case of leasing, it can be the fund management strategy, maximum rent levels or other regulatory guidelines the players have to obey. This is true for commercial assets (office, retail, ...), but even more for residential assets. The level of regulations also depends on the country in which the asset and/or the property company/investor is located.

The game can be presented using its *normal form* or its *extensive form*. The normal form is a description of the payoffs as a function of the strategies in a *payoff matrix*, while the extensive form describes the game in more detail using a *game tree* (or *extensive form diagram*). We will come back to concrete examples of both these descriptions later on. Given strategies from the other players, the *best response* for a player is the strategy that maximises his or her payoff. If the same strategy gives the highest payoff for a player irrespectively of the other player's or players' strategies, then this strategy is said to be a *dominant strategy* for this player. A *Nash equilibrium* is a set of strategies such that given the other player's or players' strategies, no player wants to change his or her strategy. Nash equilibrium is the main equilibrium concept used in game theory. Dominant strategies and Nash equilibria are linked together, as the following result shows.

> **Dominant strategies and Nash equilibria**
>
> If each player in a game has a dominant strategy, then this a Nash equilibrium. On the other hand, a Nash equilibrium need not be of the form of a dominant strategy for each player.

Examples of Nash equilibria that contain dominant strategies for both players, a dominant strategy for only one of the players and equilibria where none of the players has a dominant strategy will be presented later on in this chapter.

2.2 Static games

In a *static game*, the game is played exactly once. The players have *complete information* about the payoffs of all the players, but have *incomplete information* regarding the actions of other players. We often describe a static game by using the normal form of a game. One example is given in Figure 2.1

		Player A	
		Strategy I	**Strategy II**
Player B	Strategy I	(1,1)	(0,3)
	Strategy II	(3,2)	(2,2)

Figure 2.1: Normal form of a static game.

Here, the (x_A, x_B) in the payoff matrix of the normal form description of the game means that Player A gets the payoff x_A, and Player B the payoff x_B. We have emphasised that Player A's payoff is the first of the components and Player B's the second by using bold face and sans serif respectively. To analyse this game, we look at each of the players at a time, and determine their respective best responses. Let us start with Player A. If Player B chooses Strategy I, then Player A gets the payoff 1 if Strategy I is chosen, and gets 0 if Strategy II is chosen. Since $1 > 0$, we can conclude that

> Player A will choose Strategy I if Player B chooses strategy I.

If Player B chooses Strategy II, then Player A gets the payoff 3 if Strategy I is chosen, and gets 2 if Strategy II is chosen. Since $3 > 2$, we can conclude that

> Player A will choose Strategy I if Player B chooses strategy II.

Hence, irrespectively of if Player B chooses Strategy I or Strategy II, Player A will choose Strategy I. This means that *Strategy I is a dominant strategy for Player A in this game*. Turning to Player B, we see that if Player A chooses Strategy I, then Player B gets the payoff 1 if Strategy I is chosen, and gets 2 if Strategy II is chosen. Since $2 > 1$, we can conclude that

> Player B will choose Strategy II if Player A chooses strategy I.

Furthermore, if Player A chooses Strategy II, then Player B gets the payoff 3 if Strategy I is chosen, and gets 2 if Strategy II is chosen. Since $3 > 2$, we can conclude that

> Player B will choose Strategy I if Player A chooses strategy II.

This means that Player B will choose different strategies depending on the choice of strategy by Player A. Hence, *there exists no dominant strategy for Player B in this game*. This means that there is no Nash equilibrium in this game where each player has a dominant strategy. What about a Nash equilibrium without dominant strategies for all players? We claim that

> *Player A choosing Strategy I and Player B choosing Strategy II is a Nash equilibrium in this game.*

To show this, we assume that Player B chooses Strategy II. Since Strategy I is a dominant strategy for Player A, Player A will (always) choose Strategy I. If, on the other hand, Player A chooses Strategy I, then we know from above that Player B will choose Strategy II. This shows that *given the other player's strategy, it is optimal to choose according to the strategies above.* Hence, choosing these strategies is a Nash equilibrium.

2.2.1 Prisoner's dilemma

The prisoner's dilemma is one of the most classic examples of a static game. Typical payoffs of the normal form of this type of game are given in Figure 2.2.

To analyse this game, we start by looking at the best responses for each of the players.

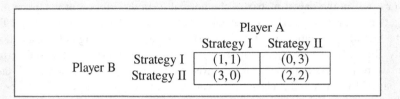

Figure 2.2: Prisoner's dilemma.

For Player A:

- Player B chooses Strategy I → Player A chooses Strategy I.
  In this case, Player A gets 1 and Player B gets 1.

- Player B chooses Strategy II → Player A chooses Strategy I.
  In this case, Player A gets 3 and Player B gets 0.

For Player B:

- Player A chooses Strategy I → Player B chooses Strategy I.
  In this case, Player A gets 1 and Player B gets 1.

- Player A chooses Strategy II → Player B chooses Strategy I.
  In this case, Player A gets 0 and Player B gets 3.

Hence, whichever strategy Player B uses, Player A chooses Strategy I. This means that always choosing Strategy I is a dominant strategy for Player A. In the same way, Player B always chooses Strategy I irrespectively of what Player A chooses, so choosing Strategy I is a dominant strategy also for Player B. It follows that

Player A choosing Strategy I and Player B choosing Strategy I is a dominant strategy for both players, and hence also (the only) Nash equilibrium in this game.

We can use this set-up to model the competition between two property developers. In this case, $(1, 1)$ are the payoffs when the two firms compete, and $(2, 2)$ is the payoff if they form a cartel. If they work together in a cartel, then they will increase their profits compared with the situation when they compete. In order to fully analyse this situation we need to use oligopoly models, which are the theme of Chapter 3, and we will return to the two property developers there.

2.2.2 Stag hunt

The game with the normal form as in Figure 2.3 is called the stag hunt game.

For this game the best responses are given below.

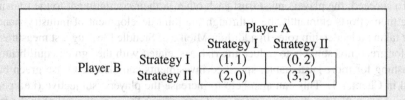

		Player A	
		Strategy I	Strategy II
Player B	Strategy I	$(1, 1)$	$(0, 2)$
	Strategy II	$(2, 0)$	$(3, 3)$

Figure 2.3: Stag hunt game.

For Player A:

- Player B chooses Strategy I → Player A chooses Strategy I.
  In this case, Player A gets 1 and Player B gets 1.

- Player B chooses Strategy II → Player A chooses Strategy II.
  In this case, Player A gets 3 and Player B gets 3.

For Player B:

- Player A chooses Strategy I → Player B chooses Strategy I.
  In this case, Player A gets 1 and Player B gets 1.

- Player A chooses Strategy II → Player B chooses Strategy II.
  In this case, Player A gets 3 and Player B gets 3.

First of all we notice that there is no dominant strategy for either of the players. On the other hand

Player A choosing Strategy I and Player B choosing Strategy I and Player A choosing Strategy II and Player B choosing Strategy II are two Nash equilibria.

The stag hunt game can be illustrated by the real estate industry's transition to more circular, sustainable operations (DeCanio & Fremstad [10]). Until now, industry actors could and can in many cases still make a profit by building or selling "brown" buildings, i.e., buildings with high operational carbon emissions and embodied carbon in the material used (payoff: $(1, 1)$ – i.e., a "brown [Nash] equilibrium" Mielke & Steudle [36]). Trying to adopt more practices as a single actor in the industry will, however, be challenging. Not only does it come with extensive R&D investments and financial risks, but also the supporting structures are missing. Take for example the transition to a more circular material use. A developer on its own does neither dispose of a large physical material bank (beyond its own property portfolio), nor of a platform to match existing building components to new project designs, nor of the legal framework and certainties that the use of these materials will be approved by surveyors and investors. The payoff $(0, 2)$ of a circular building strategy will hence in many cases be lower than for actors sticking to traditional approaches.

However, an ecosystem transformation, where several actors collectively push for more circular structures and the use of renewable energies, will ultimately increase the payoff for all parties involved ($(3, 3)$ – i.e., a "green [Nash] equilibrium" Mielke & Steudle [36]). Hence, real estate investors and developers, platform providers and the industry at large all contribute to a sustainable built environment. Here, the risks are shared among more players, sustainable technologies reach maturity faster, and new business models emerge and contribute to growing the overall market volume. To succeed, the players must trust each other in their commitment to the transition and coordinate their efforts efficiently, be it through the joint development of industry standards or one player taking a leadership role. In addition, Mielke & Steudle [36] suggest measures such as subsidies for green investments to reduce the risk associated with the "green equilibrium". One way of pushing for more sustainable, specified investments can also be to use green bonds, as introduced in Chapter 1. This can also help to increase the players' subjective (i.e., perceived) probability of other players choosing green, as it strengthens the common belief in the transition and future profits from green investment.

2.2.3   Chicken game

The last of our example games is the chicken game. The normal form of this game is given in Figure 2.4. Again, we start by looking at the best responses for each of the players.

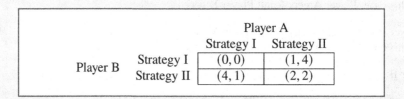

Figure 2.4: Chicken game.

For Player A:

- Player B chooses Strategy I → Player A chooses Strategy II.
  In this case, Player 1 gets X and Player B gets 4.

- Player B chooses Strategy II → Player A chooses Strategy I.
  In this case, Player A gets 4 and Player B gets 1.

For Player B:

- Player A chooses Strategy I → Player B chooses Strategy II.
  In this case, Player A gets 4 and Player B gets 1.

- Player A chooses Strategy II → Player B chooses Strategy I.
  In this case, Player A gets 1 and Player B gets 4.

In this game, there is no dominant strategy for any of the players, but, as in the stag hunt game, there are two Nash equilibria.

Player A choosing Strategy I and Player B choosing Strategy II and Player A choosing Strategy II and Player B choosing Strategy I are the two Nash equilibria.

To understand the chicken game, let us take a closer look at the leasing example introduced in Section 2.1. Both parties are worst off if they both choose to defeat, i.e., not to compromise (payoff $(0,0)$). No lease agreement is made and hence the landlord misses rental income while the tenant does not get to use the office (or retail, logistics, ...) space. For their individual best outcome, each party will want to do the opposite of what the opponent does: if the landlord is willing to compromise, the tenant will get the best deal by not giving in and vice versa (payoff $(1, 4)$ or $(4, 1)$). Both of these states are equilibria, but it will be difficult to predict in advance which of them will be reached. This depends on the expectations of the two parties about the negotiation behaviour of the respective counterpart. However, this would lead to many negotiations failing in practice. Therefore, if both parties are willing to compromise $(2, 2)$, an agreement is probably reached. For more elaborations on this case, continue reading in the dynamic games section.

2.3 Dynamic games

A game that is played more than once is said to be a *dynamic game*. A dynamic game can either be *repeated* or *sequential*. In a repeated game, a static game is played several times, either a finite or an inifinite number of times. It could also be repeated a random number of times. The previous moves of every player are known to the other players; we say that there is *almost perfect information*. In a sequential game, the players make their choices one at a time. The previous moves of the players are known when a player chooses his or her action – in this case there is *perfect information*. In Figure 2.5 is an example of a sequential game in its extensive form. In this

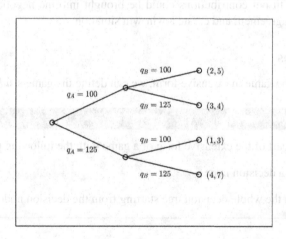

Figure 2.5: Sequential game structure.

dynamic game, Player A starts by choosing his or her quantity q_A; in this case there are only the two choices $q_A = 100$ or $q_A = 125$. After Player A has made his or her choice, Player B choose quantity q_B, which in this game is either $q_B = 100$ or $q_B = 125$. Note that there is also a normal form of this game, depicted in Figure 2.6, but in the normal form description the fact that Player A moves first needs to be explicitly stated, as the ordinary payoff matrix does not contain this information. Also note that it is easier to solve for the equilibrium (or equilibria) in a sequential game by using the extensive form.

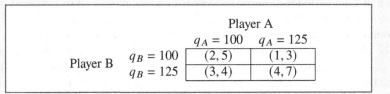

		Player A	
		$q_A = 100$	$q_A = 125$
Player B	$q_B = 100$	(2, 5)	(1, 3)
	$q_B = 125$	(3, 4)	(4, 7)

Figure 2.6: Normal form of a sequential game.

The above-mentioned negotiations of lease contracts are often not a static one-off event in reality, but rather a dynamic, iterative process. Here, one party's action is a reaction to its opponent's last move (i.e., it is a sequential game). If one party does not offer any concessions while the other is constantly compliant, the danger exists that the latter ends its willingness to compromise, to the effect that the negotiations fail. As both parties can punish unwanted behaviour of their opponent and (threaten to) end negotiations, it is in the actors' best interest to compromise; see Pfrang & Wittig [44]. See also the section on folk theorems in Section 2.3.3. Note that "compromise" in this example does not only imply an agreement about the rent level. Instead, more flexible lease terms (e.g., prolongation or break options) and incentives like rent-free periods or fit-out contributions could be brought into the negotiations to expand the range of a potential agreement and create a win-win situation.

2.3.1 Subgames

When we consider the game in extensive form, we can define the game's *subgames*.

Definition of a subgame

A subgame is a part of the extensive form of a game with the following properties:

- It starts at a decision node.

- It includes the whole decision tree starting from the decision node.

Figure 2.7 is a schematic description of the subgames for the game in Figure 2.5. Each oval represents a subgame, so this game has three subgames. Note that *the game itself is always a subgame*.

2.3.2 Subgame perfect Nash equilibria

When we consider dynamic games, we need to introduce a new concept of equilibrium, that of a *subgame perfect Nash equilibrium*. The definition of a subgame perfect Nash equilibrium is that there should be a Nash equilibrium *in every subgame of the game*. To find the subgame perfect equilibrium of a sequential game, we typically work backwards. Consider the game whose extensive form is depicted in Figure 2.7.

Now assume that Player A, the leader, has made his or her move. If the chosen quantity was $q_A = 100$, then Player B gets the payoff 5 if he or she chooses $q_B = 100$, and 4 if he or she

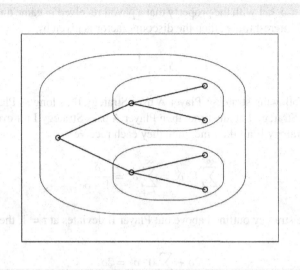

Figure 2.7: Subgames in sequential games.

chooses $q_B = 125$. Since $5 > 4$, Player B chooses $q_B = 100$ if Player A chooses $q_A = 100$. If Player A has chosen $q_A = 125$, then, by an equivalent reasoning, Player B will choose $q_B = 125$ since $7 > 3$. This is known by Player A, when he or she decides whether to choose $q_A = 100$ or $q_A = 125$. If Player A chooses $q_A = 100$, then Player B will choose $q_B = 100$, and the payoff to Player A is 2. If, on the other hand, Player A chooses $q_A = 125$, then Player B chooses $q_B = 125$, and Player A gets 4. Since $4 > 2$, Player A will choose $q_A = 125$. To summarise: The subgame perfect Nash equilibrium in the game depicted in Figure 2.5 is $(q_A, q_B) = (125, 125)$, and the payoffs are 4 to Player A and 7 to Player B.

2.3.3 Folk theorems

Consider the playing of a prisoner's dilemma type of game several times between two players. In Figure 2.8 the normal form of this game is depicted. The fact that the game is played several times means that it is a repeated game.

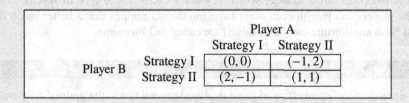

		Player A	
		Strategy I	Strategy II
Player B	Strategy I	$(0, 0)$	$(-1, 2)$
	Strategy II	$(2, -1)$	$(1, 1)$

Figure 2.8: Single game played repeatedly.

The players value a payoff higher when it occurs earlier than when it occurs later, and we introduce a *discount factor* $0 < \delta < 1$ with the property that a payoff received in game number t is multiplied by δ^t. If there is an interest rate r, then the discount factor is given by

$$\delta = \frac{1}{1+r}.$$

Now consider the following strategy: Player A uses Strategy II as long as Player B uses Strategy II. If Player B uses Strategy I at any time, then Player A uses Strategy I for ever after this time. If *both* players use Strategy II all the time, then they each receive[1]

$$\sum_{t=1}^{\infty} 1 \cdot \delta^t = \sum_{t=1}^{\infty} \delta^t = \frac{\delta}{1-\delta}.$$

If Player A uses the strategy outlined above but Player B deviates at $t = 1$, then Player B receives

$$2\delta + \sum_{t=2}^{\infty} 0 \cdot \delta^t = 2\delta.$$

This means that Player B will deviate from always using Strategy II if

$$2\delta > \frac{\delta}{1-\delta}.$$

This inequality is satisfied exactly when

$$\delta < \frac{1}{2}.$$

On the other hand, if the reversed inequality is satisfied, i.e. if

$$\delta \geq \frac{1}{2},$$

then the cost of deviating is too high for Player B, and if this condition is satisfied then Player B will *not* deviate. The same argument can be used for Player A, resulting in the same inequality. The conclusion is that if the discount factor is high enough, in this case greater or equal to $1/2$, then the threat of only getting the non-cooperative profit of 0 means that neither of the players deviate from the cooperative strategy when they get 1 each. These type of results, where the fact that the players can punish each other by using threats implies that a better result than the one-period Nash equilibrium can be sustained are called *folk theorems*.

A folk theorem

When a prisoner's dilemma type of game is played several times, the optimal cooperative solution can be sustained. In general, if this is possible, or if deviation is optimal, is dependent in a critical way on the discount factor.

---

[1]Here we use the fact that for $|a| < 1$ it holds that $\sum_{i=1}^{\infty} a^i = \frac{a}{1-a}$.

2.4 Literature notes

The classical reference to game theory is Morgenstern & von Neumann [38]. For a general introduction to game theory in the context of microeconomics on the level of this book, we refer to Perloff [43] or Varian [53]. Dixit, Skeeth & McAdams [12], Gibbons [16] and Watson [54] are books on game theory aimed at students of economics. A more applied introduction to game theory, and including other subjects raised in this book, can be found in Hendrikse [22]. Dixit & Nalebuff [11] gives an introduction to game theory at a very basic level. Kuhn & Nasar [29] contains a short biography of John F. Nash together with descriptions of his research, including a facsimile of his PhD thesis from Princeton where the concept of what is now called a Nash equilibrium was introduced.

2.5 Exercises

Exercise 2.1 Consider the following game:

		Player A	
		I	II
Player B	I	$(2, 3)$	$(10, -5)$
	II	$(8, 9)$	$(7, 7)$

a) Find the best responses for each player in this game.

b) How many Nash equilibria are there?

Exercise 2.2 Consider the following game:

		Player A	
		I	II
Player B	I	$(-2, 4)$	$(1, 2)$
	II	$(0, -3)$	$(5, 3)$

What are the payoffs at the (unique) Nash equilibrium?

Exercise 2.3 Firm A can choose between producing the quantities $q_A = 1$ or $q_A = 3$, and Firm B can choose between producing the quantities $q_B = 1$, $q_B = 2$ or $q_B = 3$. The payoffs to the firms are described in the game tree below. What are the payoffs to the firms in the subgame perfect Nash equilibrium in this game?

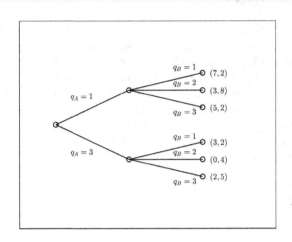

Exercise 2.4 The following game is played inifinitely many times. For which values on the discount factor is a cooperative equilibrium viable?

		Player A	
		Strategy I	Strategy II
Player B	Strategy I	$(0, 0)$	$(-2, 5)$
	Strategy II	$(5, -2)$	$(3, 3)$

Part II

Market perspective

Chapter 3

Oligopolies

In this chapter we introduce the market form oligopoly, which is when there exists more than one firm in the market, but not so many that we can consider the market as being a perfectly competitive one. We look at different oligopoly models, and also study the market form monopolistic competition. It provides answers to how different firms, e.g., construction equipment providers or real estate developers, should structure their product or service offerings in relation to their competitors. The focus here is mainly on existing market actors and their interactions.

3.1   Introduction

An *oligopoly* is a market form with a finite, but more than one number of firms. A market with only one producer is a monopoly; a market model which was studied in Section 1.3. Assuming that all firms in an oligopoly market produce the same good (this is not necessary to assume, and we will look at the generalisation where the goods are different), we have summarised the properties of different market forms in Table 3.1.

Table 3.1: Properties of three important market forms.

Type of market	Number of firms	Price	Total output	Profit per firm in the long run
Monopoly	1	High	Low	> 0
Oligopoly	≥ 2	?	?	?
Competive market	Many	Low	High	0

The question marks represents properties of the oligopoly models that we do not have an answer to now, but that will be given in this chapter. In each oligopoly model the firms compete by

49

choosing, e.g., how much to produce or which price to set on the good it produces. In this case, the quantity and price, respectively, is called the *strategic variable*. Here we collect the different types of oligopoly models that will be considered later on.

Table 3.2: Model names and their respective strategic variable.

Model	Strategic variable
Cournot	Quantity
Bertrand	Price
Stackelberg	Quantity or price

3.2 Cournot models

3.2.1 Symmetric Cournot models

In the class of *Cournot models*, the firms in an oligopoly compete by setting the quantity they will produce.

> **Properties of symmetric Cournot models**
>
> - There are $n \geq 2$ number of firms.
>
> - The firms are identical, i.e. they produce identical goods, and they all have the same cost function C.
>
> - The firms compete by choosing which quantity to produce, i.e. the strategic variable is quantity, and the firms act independently, simultaneously and with full information except about the move of the other firm; i.e. the set-up of a static game.

By "symmetric" we mean that the firms *produce the same good*, and that they *have the same cost function*. To find the optimal quantity of each of the firms, we use the idea of a Nash equilibrium: Given that my opponents behave optimally, how should I behave? We start with looking at the symmetric case with two firms.

3.2.2 Symmetric Cournot duopoly

When there are only two firms, the market form is referred to as a *duopoly*. Focusing on two firms we see that the profit of Firm 1 is

$$\pi_1 = p(Q)q_1 - C(q_1) = p(q_1 + q_2)q_1 - C(q_1),$$

and the profit of Firm 2 is

$$\pi_2 = p(Q)q_2 - C(q_2) = p(q_1 + q_2)q_2 - C(q_2).$$

Now, let us look at the profit maximising condition for each of the two firms *given the quantity of the other firm*. For Firm 1, this means that the firm wants to find the quantity q_1 such that[1]

$$\pi_1'(q_1) = p'(q_1 + q_2)q_1 + p(q_1 + q_2) - C'(q_1) = 0.$$

In the same way, the profit maximising condition for Firm 2, given the produced amount q_1 of Firm 1, is

$$\pi_2'(q_2) = p'(q_1 + q_2)q_2 + p(q_1 + q_2) - C'(q_2) = 0.$$

In order to get explicit expressions of the respective quantities, we now make the following standard assumptions.

Standard assumptions

- The inverse demand function is linear:

$$p(Q) = a - bQ$$

  for some $a, b > 0$.

- The cost function is given by

$$C(q) = cq$$

  for some $0 < c < a$.

Under the standard assumptions we have

$$p'(Q) = -b \quad \text{and} \quad C'(q) = c.$$

It follows that the profit maximising conditions are

$$-bq_1 + a - b(q_1 + q_2) - c = 0$$

and

$$-bq_2 + a - b(q_1 + q_2) - c = 0.$$

Solving for q_1 in the first equation, and for q_2 in the second yields

$$q_1 = \frac{a - c}{2b} - \frac{q_2}{2} = R_1(q_2)$$

and

$$q_2 = \frac{a - c}{2b} - \frac{q_1}{2} = R_2(q_1),$$

respectively. The functions R_1 and R_2 are the *reaction functions* or the *best-response functions*. It tells the firms how much to produce given the other firm's production level. By solving the system of equations

$$\begin{cases} q_1 &= \dfrac{a - c}{2b} - \dfrac{q_2}{2} \\[2mm] q_2 &= \dfrac{a - c}{2b} - \dfrac{q_1}{2} \end{cases}$$

---

[1]The functions π_1 and π_2 are really functions of the two variables q_1 and q_2, so we should use partial derivatives. To keep the notation short, we will, however, not use partial derivatives in this chapter when we take derivatives of profit functions.

we get

$$\begin{cases} q_1 &= \dfrac{a-c}{3b} \\[2ex] q_2 &= \dfrac{a-c}{3b}. \end{cases}$$

This is the intersection of the reaction functions in Figure 3.1. We will now show the following:

Nash equilibrium in the symmetric Cournot duopoly

The quantities

$$q_1 = \frac{a-c}{3b} \quad \text{and} \quad q_2 = \frac{a-c}{3b}$$

constitutes a Nash equilibrium.

To show this, we fix the quantity $q_2 = \frac{a-c}{3b}$ of Firm 2. In this case the optimal quantity of Firm 1 is

$$q_1 = R_1\left(\frac{a-c}{3b}\right) = \frac{a-c}{2b} - \frac{\frac{a-c}{3b}}{2} = \frac{a-c}{3b},$$

which is the quantity for Firm 1 given in the claim. In the same way we get that the optimal quantity for Firm 2 if Firm 1 produces $q_1 = \frac{a-c}{3b}$ is

$$q_2 = R_2\left(\frac{a-c}{3b}\right) = \frac{a-c}{2b} - \frac{\frac{a-c}{3b}}{2} = \frac{a-c}{3b}.$$

Again, this is the amount produced by Firm 2 according to the claim. This shows that $(q_1, q_2) = \left(\frac{a-c}{3b}, \frac{a-c}{3b}\right)$ is indeed a Nash equilibrium. In this setting, the equilibrium is also referred to as a *Nash-Cournot equilibrium* or a *Cournot equilibrium*.

Example 3.2.1 Two property developers are producing the same type of housing property and have the same cost function (in thousands of euros)

$$C(q) = 2,000q.$$

The inverse demand function is given by

$$p(Q) = 14,000 - Q.$$

Using the derived formula above, the optimal quantity of each of the companies in a Nash-Cournot equilibrium is given by

$$q_1 = q_2 = \frac{14,000 - 2,000}{3} = 4,000.$$

The profit of each of the firms ($i = 1, 2$) is

$$\begin{aligned} \pi_i &= pq_i - C(q_i) = (a - bQ)q_i - cq_i \\ &= (14,000 - 1 \cdot (4,000 + 4,000)) \cdot 4,000 - 2,000 \cdot 4,000 \\ &= 16,000,000. \end{aligned}$$

In Figure 3.1 we have plotted the reaction functions and the optimal quantities in this example.

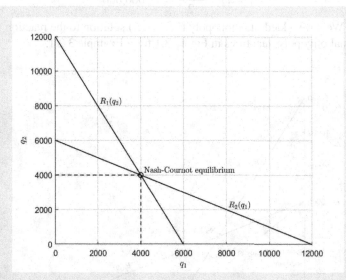

Figure 3.1: Reaction functions and optimal quantities in a symmetric Cournot duopoly.

3.2.3 Cartels

If the firms in an oligopoly instead of competing choose to cooperate, they form a *cartel*. This effectively means that the firms create a monopoly.

Example 3.2.2 Let us return to Example 3.2.1. If the firms form a cartel, thus creating a monopoly, then the combined firm behaves like a monopolist and wants to maximise

$$\pi(Q) = p(Q)Q - C(Q) = (14{,}000 - Q)Q - 2{,}000Q.$$

Letting Q_M denote the optimal total quantity of the cartel, we get the profit maximising condition (which is the same as requiring $MR(Q_M) = MC(Q_M)$)

$$\pi'(Q_M) = 14{,}000 - Q_M - Q_M - 2{,}000 = 0 \iff 12{,}000 = 2Q_M \implies Q_M = 6{,}000.$$

The price set by the cartel is

$$p_M = 14{,}000 - Q_M = 14{,}000 - 6{,}000 = 8{,}000,$$

and the total profit is

$$\pi_{\text{Total}} = (14{,}000 - 6{,}000)6{,}000 - 2{,}000 \cdot 6{,}000 = 36{,}000{,}000.$$

It follows that if the bargaining power of the two firms is equal, then each of the firms get half the profit each, i.e.

$$\pi_1 = \pi_2 = \frac{\pi_{Total}}{2} = 18,000,000$$

in this case. We have added the monopoly (i.e. cartel) solution to the reaction functions and the optimal oligopoly quantities in Figure 3.1 from Example 3.2.1.

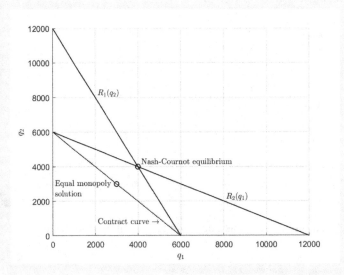

Figure 3.2: Reaction functions and optimal quantities – I.

All possible combinations of q_1 and q_2 such that $q_1 + q_2 = Q_M = 6,000$ is sometimes referred to as the *contract curve*.

The total profit is higher than the total profit for the oligopoly, but there are still problems for the cartel. One is that a firm in a cartel has incentives to deviate and produce more than the other member(s) of the cartel. The other is that the total profit needs to be shared among the firms in the cartel, and the fraction each of the firms in the cartel gets of the total profit needs to be negotiated.

3.2.4 Symmetric general Cournot oligopoly model

We now consider the case of a symmetric Cournot model (recall that this means that the firms produce the same good and has the same cost function) where there are $n \geq 2$ number of firms. This means that Firm i, $i = 1, 2, \ldots, n$, wants to maximise the profit

$$\pi_i = p(Q)q_i - cq_i,$$

where

$$Q = q_1 + \ldots + q_n$$

is the total quantity produced by all firms. We work, as above, under the standard assumptions. Now the profit function for Firm i can be written

$$\pi_i = \left(a - b(q_1 + \ldots + q_n)\right)q_i - cq_i.$$

Note that q_i is present three times in this expression:

$$\pi_i = \left(a - b(q_1 + \ldots + \boxed{q_i} + \ldots + q_n)\right) \cdot \boxed{q_i} - c \cdot \boxed{q_i}.$$

The quantities per firm, the total quantity produced, the price and the profit per firm is given by (for a proof of these expressions, see Appendix A.4):

Overview: The symmetric general Cournot model

- Quantity per firm:
$$q = \frac{a - c}{b(n + 1)}.$$

- Market quantity:
$$Q = n\frac{a - c}{b(n + 1)}.$$

- Price:
$$p = \frac{a + cn}{n + 1}.$$

- Profit per firm:
$$\pi = b\left(\frac{a - c}{n + 1}\right)^2.$$

We end this section by considering what happens if the number of firms increases more and more. Mathematically this means that $n \to \infty$. Applying this to the formulas for the quantities shows that

$$q \to 0 \text{ and } Q \to \frac{a - c}{b}.$$

For the price it holds that

$$p \to c = MC(q)$$

and the profit per firm goes to zero:

$$\pi \to 0.$$

But we see that the total profit of all firms $\pi_{\text{Total}} = n\pi$ also goes to zero:

$$\pi_{\text{Total}} \to 0.$$

These findings on the market level (i.e. for the variables Q, p and π_{Total}) are consistent with a competitive market with demand function

$$Q = D(p) = \frac{a}{b} - \frac{1}{b} \cdot p.$$

3.2.5 Asymmetric Cournot models

There are two ways in which we can deviate from the symmetric Cournot model:

- The firms have different cost functions.

- The firms produces different goods.

Each of these generalisations will make the analysis of the oligopoly model more flexible, but also more complicated from a mathematical point of view. We will not pursue this path, but refer to the exercises of this chapter, which includes some examples of these types of models.

3.3 Bertrand models

In a *Bertrand model* of an oligopoly, the price, and not the quantity as in Cournot oligopoly models, is the strategic variable. It turns out that this dramatically changes the result in symmetric oligopoly models. Let us start with the same assumptions as we used when studying the Cournot duopoly.

Properties of symmetric Bertrand models

- There are $n \geq 2$ number of firms.

- The firms are identical, i.e. they produce identical goods, and they all have the same cost function C.

- The firms compete by choosing which price to set on the good they produce, i.e. the strategic variable is price, and the firms act independently, simultaneously and with full information except about the move of the other firm; i.e. the set-up of a static game.

In this case the quantity produced by Firm 1 is

$$q_1(p_1, p_2) = \begin{cases} D(p_1) & \text{if} \quad p_1 < p_2 \\ \frac{1}{2}D(p_1) & \text{if} \quad p_1 = p_2 \\ 0 & \text{if} \quad p_1 > p_2, \end{cases}$$

where $D(p)$ is the market's demand function. This function, when the demand function $D(p)$ is linear, is depicted in Figure 3.3. Why does it look like this? If Firm 1 sets a strictly lower price than Firm 2, then everyone will buy from Firm 1. In the same way, if Firm 1 sets a price strictly higher than Firm 2, then no one will buy from Firm 2. If they set the same price, then they will share the quantity produced 50/50.

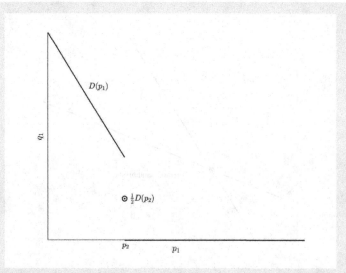

Figure 3.3: Demand functions for Bertrand competition in oligopoly markets.

In this model we have the following surprising result:

> **The Bertrand equilibrium**
>
> The equilibrium is for both firms to set their price equal to their common marginal cost, i.e. the price of both firms is pushed down to the perfect competition price.

Why is this true? First of all note that $p_1 = p_2 = c$ implies that

$$\pi_i = p_i q_i - c q_i = (p_i - c) q_i = 0 \text{ for Firm } i = 1, 2.$$

Now assume that Firm 2 sets $p_2 = c$. If Firm 1 chooses $p_1 < p_2 = c$ then Firm 1's profit is

$$\pi_1 = p_1 q_1 - c q_1 = (p_1 - c) q_1 < 0.$$

Hence, Firm 1 doesn't set $p_1 < p_2$. If Firm 1 chooses $p_1 > p_2$, then, since the two firms produce the same goods, it gets no customers and earns zero profit. But then Firm 1 can as well set $p_1 = p_2 = c$. In the same way we argue that if Firm 1 chooses $p_1 = c$, then Firm 2 should choose $p_2 = p_1 = c$. It follows that

$$(p_1, p_2) = (c, c) \text{ is a Nash equilibrium.}$$

One might think that this is just as reasonable as the outcome in the symmetric Cournot case, but it is actually an unintuitive result. If we denote the profit per firm in a Cournot model with n firms by π_n for $n \geq 2$, then we saw that $\pi_n \to 0$ as n increases. I.e., the more firms on the market, the lower is the profit per firm, and as the number of firms goes to infinity, the profit goes

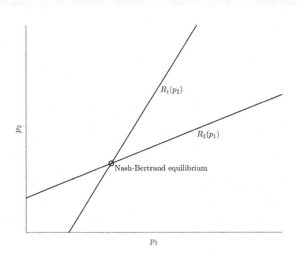

Figure 3.4: Reaction functions for Bertrand competition in oligopoly markets.

to zero. This is a behaviour we expect – as $n \to \infty$ the model "looks like" a competitive market. The Nash-Bertrand equilibrium with identical products has zero profit already when $n = 2$.

Does this mean that the Bertrand model is useless? No, it means that we have to change some assumption(s). By assuming that the products are differentiated, we can get "reasonable" results from Bertrand models, i.e. when we use price as the strategic variable. In this case the reaction functions are *upward sloping*. See Figure 3.4 for an illustration of this. Exercise 3.5 contains an example of this kind of model.

3.4   Stackelberg models

The Cournot model can be considered as a game that is played once, i.e. it is a static game. In some cases there is a leading firm which sets its quantity or price, and then one or more firms see this quantity or price and react to it. These type of oligopoly models, where there is a *leader* and *follower* are called *Stackelberg models*, and is an example of a sequential dynamic game. We will only consider Stackelberg models with two firms who use quantity as the strategic variable, and we let Firm 1 be the leader and Firm 2 the follower. We also use the standard assumptions above.

As usual we start by analysing the dynamic game backwards, i.e. we start with Firm 2. For Firm 2, the quantity q_1 chosen by Firm 1 is now known, and this leads to the maximisation problem

$$\pi_2(q_2) = p(Q)q_2 - C(q_2) = p(q_1 + q_2)q_2 - cq_2.$$

But this is *exactly* the same lem Firm 2 faces in the Cournot model, so we know that the solution is

$$q_2 = \frac{a - c}{2b} - \frac{q_1}{2}. \tag{3.1}$$

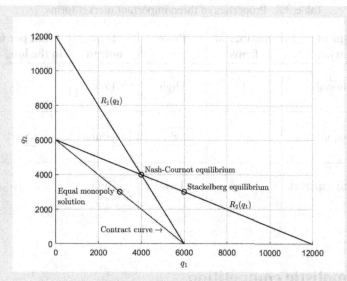

Figure 3.5: Reaction functions and optimal quantities – II.

Now comes the difference between the Cournot and Stackelberg models: When Firm 1 chooses its quantity q_1, it *knows* that if it chooses q_1, then Firm 2 will choose q_2 according to the formula in Equation (3.1). This is used by Firm 1 when writing its profit function:

$$\begin{aligned} \pi_1(q_1) &= p(Q)q_1 - C(q_1) \\ &= (a - b(q_1 + q_2))q_1 - cq_1 \\ &= \left(a - b\left(q_1 + \frac{a-c}{2b} - \frac{q_1}{2}\right)\right)q_1 - cq_1 \\ &= \left(a - b\frac{q_1}{2} - \frac{a-c}{2}\right)q_1 - cq_1. \end{aligned}$$

Taking the derivative of this and setting it to zero in order to find the optimal quantity q_1 results in the equation

$$\pi_1'(q_1) = a - b\frac{q_1}{2} - \frac{a-c}{2} - b\frac{q_1}{2} - c = 0.$$

This simplifies to

$$bq_1 = \frac{a-c}{2} \quad \Rightarrow \quad q_1 = \frac{a-c}{2b}.$$

With this quantity chosen by Firm 1, it is optimal for Firm 2 to choose its quantity according to Equation (3.1):

$$q_2 = \frac{a-c}{2b} - \frac{1}{2} \cdot \frac{a-c}{2b} = \frac{a-c}{4b}.$$

The Stackelberg quantities are added to the quantities in the other market forms in Figure 3.5.

Concluding notes on oligopolies

Returning to the table from the beginning of the chapter, we can now replace the question marks that were present there.

Table 3.3: Properties of three important market forms.

Type of market	Number of firms	Price	Total output	Profit per firm in the long run
Monopoly	1	High	Low	> 0
Oligopoly	≥ 2	Medium	Medium	≥ 0
Competive market	Many	Low	High	0

3.5 Monopolistic competition

Although not formally a model of oligopoly, the market model *monopolistic competition* is an important model, and close to the oligopoly. This type of market has the following characteristics:

Properties of monopolistic competition models

- There are n number of firms.

- Each firm produce a unique good, but the goods are very close substitutes.

- It is easy for firms to enter and exit the market.

We will additionally assume the following:

1) The goods are so close substitutes that the inverse demand function of each of the good is given by:
$$p_i(q_i) = a - b(q_1 + q_2 + \ldots + q_n) = a - bQ$$
for some $a, b > 0$.

2) The firms have the same cost function
$$C(q) = cq + F$$
for some $0 < c < a$ and $F > 0$.

Since the firms produce unique goods, each firm behaves as a monopolist, and wants to find the quantity q_i such that
$$\pi_i = p(q_1 + \ldots + p_n)q_i - C(q_i) = \left(a - b(q_1 + \ldots + q_n)\right)q_i - (cq_i + F)$$
is maximised. We prove the following in Appendix A.5.

> **Overview: Equilibrium in monopolistic competition**
>
> - The firms each produce the same quantity
>
> $$q = \frac{a - c}{b(n + 1)}.$$
>
> - The price of the good produced by the firms is the same, and given by
>
> $$p = \frac{a + nc}{n + 1}.$$
>
> - Each firm makes the profit
>
> $$\pi = \frac{(a - c)^2}{b(n + 1)^2} - F.$$

We note that in this model the marginal revenue (the same for every firm) is given by

$$MR(q) = a - bQ - bq - c \quad \Leftrightarrow \quad MR(q) = a - c - b(n + 1)q.$$

Example 3.5.1 Consider the model above with

$$a = 80, \quad b = 1, \quad c = 20 \text{ and } F = 225.$$

In the table below we have listed the profit as a function of the number of firms n for these parameter values.

Number of firms n	1	2	3	4	5
Profit per firm π_i	675	175	0	-81	-125

When there is positive profit for each firm, the situation is as in Figure 3.6; recall that $\pi = q(p - AC(q))$. The possibility of free entry and exit will imply that if the profit per firm is strictly positive, then firms will enter the market, and if the profit per firm is negative, then firms will leave the market. In equilibrium, the profit for each firm will be equal to zero. This situation is depicted in Figure 3.7. Using the formula for the profit, we see that it will be zero when

$$\frac{(a - c)^2}{b(n + 1)^2} - F = 0.$$

Given all other parameters, this is an equation for the number n of firms in a market having monopolistic competition. Solving for n we get that the number of firms in equilibrium when there is monopolistic competition is given by

$$n = \frac{a - c}{\sqrt{bF}} - 1.$$

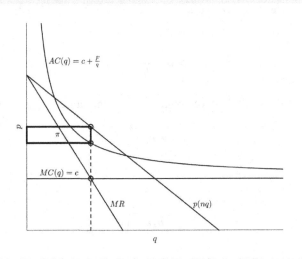

Figure 3.6: Strictly positive profit in monopolistic competition.

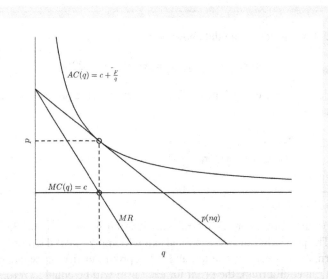

Figure 3.7: Zero profit in monopolistic competition.

3.6   Measuring market concentration

When creating a model of a market, we need to choose which type of model to use. If there is only one firm in the market, then it is natural to assume that this firm is a monopolist, but when there are more than one firm, we need to choose if the market should be modelled as an oligopoly, a market with monopolistic competition, or a market with perfect competition. If there are a few firms, then one of the two first models should probably work, but if the market has, say, 15 firms, then it could be better to model it is as a perfectly competitive market.

In order to get a better understanding of which market form best represents the market situation we face, one way is to calculate the *Herfindahl-Hirschman index* HHI. This index is defined as

$$\text{HHI} = \sum_{i=1}^{n} s_i^2,$$

where s_i, $i = 1, \ldots, n$, is the *market share* of firm i. The market share of firm i is defined as the quantity q_i the firm produces, divided by the total quantity in the market:

$$s_i = \frac{q_i}{Q} = \frac{q_i}{\sum_{j=1}^{n} q_j}.$$

Example 3.6.1 In a city there are five firms offering the rental of small residential apartments. The number of apartments each has to offer are given by

Firm	1	2	3	4	5
q_i	400	280	850	125	220

Hence, the total number of apartments is $Q = 1875$, and the market shares are

Firm	1	2	3	4	5
s_i	0.213	0.149	0.453	0.067	0.117

This results in a Herfindahl-Hirschmann index of

$$\text{HHI} = 0.213^2 + 0.149^2 + 0.453^2 + 0.067^2 + 0.117^2 = 0.29.$$

How can the Herfindahl-Hirschmann index now be used in order to determine the best model for a given market? In Horizontal Merger Guidelines [51] written by the U.S. Department of Justice and the Federal Trade Commission, they use the limits as given in Table 3.4. Note that in the Horizontal Merger Guidelines [51], the Herfindahl-Hirschmann index is caluated using the percentage as numbers, and not as decimals.

Table 3.4: Market concentration and the Herfindahl-Hirschmann index.

Market concentration	Value of HHI
Unconcentrated	HHI ≤ 0.15
Moderately concentrated	$0.15 < \text{HHI} \leq 0.25$
Highly concentrated	HHI > 0.25

3.7 Literature notes

The material in this chapter can be found in essentially any intermediate economics book such as Perloff [43] or Varian [53].

3.8 Exercises

Exercise 3.1 Two construction material suppliers in the US offer the same type of structural timber elements. The common cost function is

$$C(q) = 3q$$

and the inverse demand function is

$$p(Q) = 10 - Q.$$

a) How much timber is produced by each firm if they compete by choosing their optimal quantity?

b) How much is produced in total if the firms create a cartel?

c) How does an increase in raw material prices and supply chain challenges, resulting in the new cost function

$$C(q) = 4q$$

affect the optimal outcome in both cases?

Exercise 3.2 Consider the two companies in Exercise 3.1. This time, they still produce the same good, but have different cost functions because of their abilities to deal with supply chain interruptions. For Firm 1, this is

$$C_1(q) = 2q$$

and for Firm 2 it is

$$C_2(q) = 4q.$$

If the inverse demand function for the good still is

$$p(Q) = 10 - Q,$$

how much will each of the firms produce?

Exercise 3.3 Show that $q_1 = q_2 = \ldots = q_n$ in the symmetric Cournot model by considering Equation (A.1).

Exercise 3.4 Two construction material suppliers sell structural elements, one is specialised on timber structures, the other on bamboo structures. Assuming a similar production approach, their equal cost function is

$$C(q) = 4q.$$

The inverse demand functions for timber and bamboo structures are

$$p_1(q_1, q_2) = 10 - q_1 - q_2$$

and

$$p_2(q_1, q_2) = 18 - 2q_1 - 2q_2$$

respectively. How much is produced of each of the two goods if the two firms compete by setting their quantity?

Exercise 3.5 The two companies in Exercise 3.2 have managed to improve their production efficiency and thus reduced their cost functions to

$$C(q) = q.$$

They now perform a market analysis to better understand the overall demand for structural elements and the consumer preferences. To model the demand using a Bertrand model, the demand functions are defined as

$$D_1(p_1, p_2) = 10 - p_1 + 2p_2$$

and

$$D_2(p_1, p_2) = 5 + p_1 - p_2$$

respectively. How much is produced of each of the goods?

Exercise 3.6 Assume that the market for construction cranes in Spain consists of several actors with comparable business models and product offerings. Each firm has a constant marginal cost of €5 million and a fixed cost of €8 million. If there is free entry and exit to the market and the market's inverse demand function is given by

$$p = 25 - 2Q,$$

with price in millions of euros, how many firms will be in the market in equilibrium?

Chapter 4

Strategic interactions

This chapter focuses on market entry strategies. After an introduction to reaction functions with a general action, we use an example of shopping malls and their tenants to show how companies can enter a new market, and how the companies already in the market can prevent their competitors from doing so.

4.1 Introduction

We saw in Chapter 3 on oligopolies that the reaction functions when quantity is the strategic variable are downward sloping, and that they are upward sloping when price is the strategic variable. To study these properties further, we let a_1 and a_2 denote the value of an *action* taken by Firm 1 and Firm 2 respectively, and write the profit of Firm 1 as

$$\pi_1(a_1, a_2),$$

and the profit of Firm 2 as

$$\pi_2(a_1, a_2).$$

For Firm 1 to find its optional action, it solves the equation

$$\frac{\partial \pi_1}{\partial a_1}(a_1, a_2) = 0.$$

Solving this equation for the optimal action, which will in general depend on the action a_2 of Firm 2, we get the reaction function of Firm 1:

$$a_1 = R_1(a_2).$$

In the same way, by solving

$$\frac{\partial \pi_2}{\partial a_2}(a_1, a_2) = 0.$$

for the optimal action for Firm 2, we get Firm 2's reaction function

$$a_2 = R_2(a_1).$$

At an equilibrium point we have

$$\begin{cases} a_1 &=& R_1(a_2) \\ a_2 &=& R_2(a_1). \end{cases}$$

Example 4.1.1 Two large hotel operators compete in a national market for budget hotels. In order to get a larger share of the market, the two firms can advertise. The total value of the target market is M, and the part of the value of the market each firm gets is equal to M times the proportion of the total amount each of the two firms invest in advertisements. If Firm 1 invests the amount a_1 in advertisements, and Firm 2 the amount a_2, then the net value of advertising for Firm 1 is

$$M \cdot \frac{a_1}{a_1 + a_2} - a_1,$$

and

$$M \cdot \frac{a_2}{a_1 + a_2} - a_2$$

for Firm 2. In order to determine the reaction function for each firm (and the Nash equilibrium), we look at the optimal value for Firm 1, given that the amount a_2 is used by Firm 2. The first-order condition for Firm 1 is

$$M \cdot \frac{1 \cdot (a_1 + a_2) - a_1 \cdot 1}{(a_1 + a_2)^2} - 1 = 0.$$

This can be written

$$M \cdot \frac{a_2}{(a_1 + a_2)^2} = 1,$$

from which it follows that

$$M a_2 = (a_1 + a_2)^2.$$

Since each firm only can invest a positive amount in advertising, we have $a_1, a_2 \geq 0$, so taking the square root of the latest equation yields

$$\sqrt{M a_2} = a_1 + a_2.$$

Hence,

$$a_1 = \sqrt{M a_2} - a_2,$$

and the reaction function for Firm 1 is given by

$$R_1(a_2) = \sqrt{M a_2} - a_2.$$

Since the model is symmetric regarding Firm 1 and Firm 2, we will get that the optimal amount for Firm 2, given that the amount used by Firm 1 is a_1, is

$$a_2 = \sqrt{M a_1} - a_1,$$

and that the reaction function for Firm 2 is

$$R_2(a_1) = \sqrt{M a_1} - a_1.$$

See Figure 4.1 for a depiction of them.

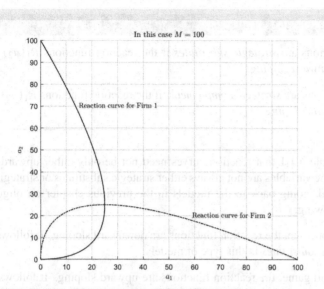

Figure 4.1: Non-linear reaction functions.

To find a Nash equilibrium we want to solve the system of equations

$$\begin{cases} a_1 &= R_1(a_2) \\ a_2 &= R_2(a_1). \end{cases}$$

By using symmetry, we find that the firms will use the same amount a on advertisements: $a_1 = a_2 = a$, and it follows that a solves

$$x = \sqrt{Ma} - a \iff 2a = \sqrt{Ma} \iff 4a^2 = Ma.$$

We see that $a = 0$ is a solution, and after dividing by a also that

$$a = \frac{M}{4}$$

is a solution. If $a = 0$, then neither of the firms advertise, and the gain from advertising is 0. If they advertise $a = M/4$ each, then they each gain

$$M \cdot \frac{M/4}{M/4 + M/4} - \frac{M}{4} = \frac{M}{2} - \frac{M}{4} = \frac{M}{4}$$

from advertising, and this choice is the optimal one.

Recall (see Section 1.2.5) that two goods 1 and 2 are substitutes if an increase in price of one of them increases the demand for the other, and are complements if an increase in price of one of them decreases the demand for the other. Inspired by this, Bulow, Geanakopols & Klemperer [6] introduced the following concepts of *strategic substitutes* and *strategic complements* for actions.

Strategic substitutes and complements

- Two actions are *strategic substitutes* if the reaction functions $R_1(a_2)$ and $R_2(a_1)$ are *downward sloping*.

- Two actions are *strategic complements* if the reaction functions $R_1(a_2)$ and $R_2(a_1)$ are *upward sloping*.

We saw in Example 4.1.1 that reaction curves need not be only either upward- or downward-sloping, so strategic variables are not always either strategic substitutes or strategic complements. On the other hand, going back to the models in the previous chapter on oligopolies, we can conclude the following:

- In a Cournot game, the reaction functions are downward sloping. It follows that *quantities are strategic substitutes* in this type of models.

- In a Bertrand game, the reaction functions are upward sloping. It follows that *prices are strategic complements* in this type of models.

4.2 Market entry strategies

4.2.1 Market conditions

So far we have considered market forms where the participating firms have no possibility of influencing the market form. In reality, there are cases when firms can influence the market form. The important thing here is how easy it is for a competitor to *enter* a market. When there is perfect competion, there is by definition no entry level – the possibility of entering and exiting the market will in the long run drive the profit of each firm down to zero.

For the rest of this chapter we will focus on the following case: An *incumbent firm* is the monopolist on a market. There is at least one *potential entrant*, who can enter the market, thus converting the market to an oligopoly. We have seen in the chapter on oligopolies, that it is better for a firm to be a monopolist than having to share the market with another firm (or, even worse, with other firms). We assume that the incumbent firm can make an investment of an amount $K \geq 0$. This is the first step in what can be seen as a type of Stackelberg game. In the second stage, a game is played between the incumbent firm and the potential entrant. An entry game of this type will have one the following solutions.

Overview: Market entry scenarios

- Entry is *blockaded*: The incumbent firm has such an advantage towards a potential entrant, that investing nothing, i.e. choosing $K = 0$, will still make the incumbent firm a monopolist.

- Entry is *deterred*: By investing an amount $K > 0$, the incumbent firm will hinder a potential entrant from entering, and the incumbent firm will maintain its monopoly position.

- Entry is *accommodated*: The incumbent firm accepts that the entrant will enter the market (typically, it is too expensive to deter the entrant), and the market becomes a duopoly. In this case $K \geq 0$.

Which of the three alternatives will be the outcome depends on the specific entry game. In these type of games, the way the investment K influences the profit of the potential entrant is crucial, and leads to the concept of *tough* and *soft* firms.

Tough and soft firms

Let π_E be the profit of the potential entrant.

- The investment K makes the incumbent firm *tough* if

$$\frac{\partial \pi_E}{\partial K} < 0.$$

- The investment K makes the incumbent firm *soft* if

$$\frac{\partial \pi_E}{\partial K} > 0.$$

4.2.2 An entry game – Part I

A company is going to rent a salesroom in a mall. The owner of the mall offers the company an exclusivity clause. The cost for this clause to be included in the contract is K, and the clause means that no other salesroom selling products similar of the ones the company is selling will be allowed to rent a salesroom in the mall. The cost for a tenant of fitting out a salesroom in the mall is C, an upfront investment any company will have to make. The game tree in this situation is in Figure 4.2. To solve this game we again work backwards. There are two decision nodes, so there are two game trees, and only one game tree where the rival firm can make a choice. At this node, when the leader has chosen not to pay the amount K, the rival firm has to decide if it wants to enter or not. The two values the rival firm has to compare between are

$$16{,}000 - C \quad \text{and} \quad 0.$$

Depending on the cost C to enter the mall, a rival firm will make different decisions:

- If

$$16{,}000 - C \geq 0 \quad \Leftrightarrow \quad C \leq 16{,}000,$$

then it is profitable for a rival firm to enter, and it will do so.

- If

$$16{,}000 - C < 0 \quad \Leftrightarrow \quad C > 16{,}000,$$

then it is not profitable for a rival firm to enter, and it will abstain from doing so.

Considering the choice of the incumbent firm, it has two parameter values to take into account.

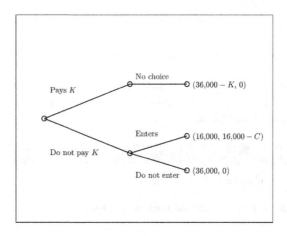

Figure 4.2: Structure of an entry game.

- If $C > 16{,}000$, then the incumbent firm has to choose between getting $36{,}000 - K$ (pay K) or $36{,}000$ (do not pay K). Since $K > 0$, the incumbent will choose not to pay, and get the payoff $36{,}000$. This is depicted in Figure 4.3. In this case, entry is blockaded.

- If $C \le 16{,}000$, then the rival firm will enter. Now the preferred strategy of the incumbent firm depends on the value of K; see the graph in Figure 4.4.

  - If $K \le 20{,}000$, then the cost of the incumbent firm is so small that it is profitable to pay K in order to hinder a rival firm from entering the mall, and entry is deterred.

  - If $K > 20{,}000$, then it is too expensive for the incumbent firm to stop the rival firm from entering, and the incumbent accepts the entry of the rival, i.e. entry is accommodated.

We can summarise the situation in this game as follows, where we have payoffs (Profit to incumbent, Profit to rival) in the matrix.

	$C \le 16{,}000$	$C > 16{,}000$
$K \le 20{,}000$	Deterred entry $(36{,}000 - K, 0)$	Blockaded entry $(36{,}000, 0)$
$K > 20{,}000$	Accommodated entry $(16{,}000, 16{,}000 - C)$	Blockaded entry $(36{,}000, 0)$

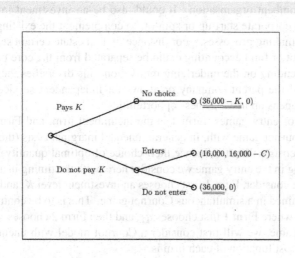

Figure 4.3: Entry is blockaded.

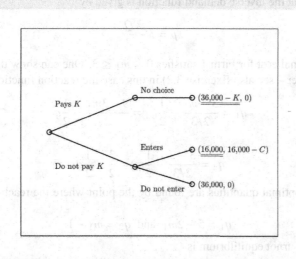

Figure 4.4: Entry is deterred or accommodated.

4.2.3 An entry game – Part II

Two firms selling the same product are competing in a Cournot game. Before the game starts, Firm 1 has the possibility of investing an amount K that will decrease its marginal cost. Such a strategic investment could for example be better technology to increase process efficiency or more precise market research to improve the product offering and sales process within the existing structures of an incumbent organisation. It could also be an investment in people or product research as part of a corporate start-up or spin-off to complement the existing product offer and streamline decision-making processes.[1] For instance, in real estate certain service offerings like property management or fund accounting could be separated from the core business units into a new company. Depending on the underlying motivation, this diversifies the risk, improves the financial structure of the parent company or allows for independent service offerings to third parties and thereby opens up new business opportunities.

In the language of entry games, Firm 1 is the incumbent firm, and Firm 2 is the potential entrant. This is a Cournot game with, in general, unequal marginal costs (the fact that they may have different fixed costs will not influence their choice of optimal quantity). It is important to distinguish the timing in the entry game we consider here, with the timing in a Stackelberg game. In the entry game we consider, Firm 1 first chooses an investment level K, and then the quantities q_1 and q_2 are determined in a simultaneous Cournot game. This is to be contrasted to the case in a Stackelberg game, where Firm 1 first chooses q_1, and then Firm 2 chooses q_2.

To analyse this game, we will first consider a Cournot model with unequal marginal costs. We assume that the cost function of each firm is

$$C_1(q_1) = m_1 q_1$$

and

$$C_2(q_2) = 2q_2$$

respectively, and that the inverse demand function is given by

$$p = 3 - \frac{Q}{3}.$$

The constant marginal cost for Firm 1 satisfies $0 \leq m_1 \leq 3$. One can show that (this is left as an exercise to the reader – see also Exercise 3.2) in this case the reaction functions are given by

$$q_1 = \frac{3 - m_1}{2/3} - \frac{1}{2}q_2 = \frac{9 - 3m_1}{2} - \frac{1}{2}q_2$$

and

$$q_2 = \frac{3 - 2}{2/3} - \frac{1}{2}q_1 = \frac{3}{2} - \frac{1}{2}q_1$$

respectively. The optimal quantities are found by the point where the reaction curves intersect, and are given by

$$q_1 = 5 - 2m_1 \quad \text{and} \quad q_2 = m_1 - 1.$$

The price at this Cournot equililbrium is

$$p = 3 - \frac{Q}{3} = 3 - \frac{q_1 + q_2}{3} = 3 - \frac{4 - m_1}{3} = \frac{5 + m_1}{3}.$$

We also need to calculate the profit of each of the firms. For Firm 1, the profit is

$$\begin{aligned} \pi_1 &= pq_1 - C(q_1) = (p - m_1)q_1 \\ &= \left(\frac{5 + m_1}{3} - m_1\right) \cdot (5 - 2m_1) \\ &= (5 - 2m_1)^2/3, \end{aligned}$$

[1]https://www.mckinsey.com/business-functions/mckinsey-digital/our-insights/the-big-boost-how-incumbents-successfully-scale-their-new-businesses

and for Firm 2

$$\begin{aligned}
\pi_2 &= pq_2 - C(q_2) = (p - m_2)q_2 \\
&= \left(\frac{5 + m_1}{3} - 2\right) \cdot (m_1 - 1) \\
&= (m_1 - 1)^2/3.
\end{aligned}$$

We summarise some of these results in Table 4.1.

Table 4.1: Impact of marginal costs on optimal quantities and profits.

	Firm 1	Firm 2
Optimal quantity	$5 - 2m_1$	$m_1 - 1$
Profit	$(5 - 2m_1)^2/3$	$(m_1 - 1)^2/3$

To continue, we study how different values of Firm 1's marginal cost m_1 influence the optimal quantities and profits for the two firms. To get the optimal quantities and profits, we use the expressions derived above with the marginal cost m_1 replaced by a numerical value.

- $m_1 = 2$: In this case the firms are identical, and the reaction functions are as the solid lines in Figure 4.5. In this case $q_1 = q_2 = 1$ and $\pi_1 = \pi_2 = 1/3$.

- $m_1 = 3/2$: Now it is cheaper for Firm 1 than for Firm 2 to produce the product. We get

$$q_1 = 2 \quad \text{and} \quad q_2 = 1/2,$$

  and the profits are

$$\pi_1 = 4/3 \quad \text{and} \quad \pi_2 = 1/12.$$

- $m_1 = 1$: Now the optimal quantity for Firm 2 has decreased to $q_2 = 0$, and thus its profit is $\pi_2 = 0$. At this point (and for all marginal costs m_1 below 1), Firm 2 has been driven out of the market, and Firm 1 is a monopolist. In this case

$$q_1 = 3 \quad \text{and} \quad \pi_1 = 3.$$

Note that when $m_1 < 1$, the formula for the optimal quantity for Firm 2 ($q_2 = m_1 - 1$) indicates that $q_2 < 0$. Since we must have $q_2 \geq 0$, this is not possible. Instead $q_2 = 0$ for every $m_1 \leq 1$. Hence, we need to be careful, and only use the formulas when they yield non-negative quantities. In Figure 4.5, the solid line represent the symmetric case with $m_1 = 2$, the dashed line is the reaction function for Firm 1 when $m_1 = 3/2$, and the dotted line is the reaction function for Firm 1 when $m_1 = 1$. The circles mark the Cournot-Nash equilibrium quantities in each of these cases. As is seen in Figure 4.5, the lower the marginal cost for Firm 1, the lower is the quantity produced by Firm 2; and when $m_1 \leq 1$, the quantity produced is zero.

We now consider the case where, by making a strategic investment, Firm 1 can lower its margin cost by making an investment of the amount $K > 0$. This investment will be costly for

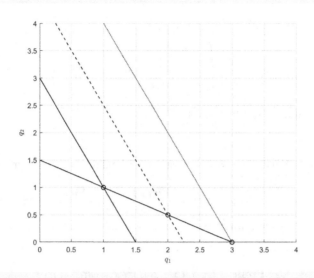

Figure 4.5: Strategic investments.

Firm 1 in the sense that it will diminish the profit of Firm 1. From a game theoretic perspective, this is a "leader-follower" game, where first Firm 1 determines the size of the capital $K \geq 0$ to be invested in order to decrease the marginal cost of Firm 1, and then the two firms play a Cournot game once. As always in sequential games, we start with the last step in the game. First, however, we need some understanding of the marginal cost $m_1(K)$ and the cost $\gamma(K)$ of making an investment of K. The marginal cost $m_1(K)$ is a decreasing function of K:

$$m_1'(K) < 0.$$

Hence, the more Firm 1 invests, the lower will its marginal cost be. The marginal cost $m_1(0)$ represents the marginal cost if no investment is done. In this model we have the following two important facts:

1) *If $m_1(0) \leq 1$, then entry is blockaded*

   By definition, entry is blockaded if, by making no investment ($K = 0$), Firm 1 will still be a monopolist (i.e. there is no entry by Firm 2). From the analysis above we know that if the marginal cost of Firm 1 is equal to or below 1, then the optimal quantity for Firm 2 is $q_2 = 0$. It follows that if $m_1(0) \leq 1$, then entry is blockaded.

2) *The investment makes Firm 1 tough*

   To see this, we start by recalling that an investment by Firm 1 (the leader) makes it tough if the profit of the potential entrant is negative, i.e. if $\partial \pi_2 / \partial K < 0$. In our model we have

   $$\frac{\partial \pi_2}{\partial K} = \frac{2(m_1(K) - 1)}{3} \cdot m_1'(K).$$

   Since $m_1'(K) < 0$, we get $\partial \pi_2 / \partial K < 0$ as long as $m_1(K) > 1$. We know that when $m_1(K) \leq 1$, then Firm 2 chooses $q_2 = 0$, i.e. $\pi_2 = 0$ when $m_1(K) \leq 1$. Hence, whenever

Firm 2 produces $q_2 > 0$, the investment makes Firm 1 tough (and when $q_2 = 0$, Firm 2 is not participating in the market).

We let $\gamma(K)$ denote the cost of investing the amount K, and we further assume that the cost of making no investment ($K = 0$) is zero, i.e. that $\gamma(0) = 0$. The cost $\gamma(K)$ is a fixed cost for Firm 1, so the profit for Firm 1 is given by the profit in the Cournot model considered above minus $\gamma(K)$:

$$\pi_1(K) = \frac{(5 - 2m_1(K))^2}{3} - \gamma(K).$$

Hence, the first-order condition with respect to K is

$$\pi_1'(K) = \frac{4}{3} \cdot (2m_1(K) - 5) \cdot m_1'(K) - \gamma'(K) = 0.$$

In order to get an understanding of how the functions $m_1(K)$ and $\gamma(K)$ influence the optimal choice of K for Firm 1, we consider the following model:

$$m_1(K) = \frac{2}{1 + K} \quad \text{and} \quad \gamma(K) = K^a$$

for a constant $a \geq 1$. By looking at different values of a, we will see how the optimal choice of K changes. We also make the simplifying assumption that K can at most be 1, i.e. that $0 \leq K \leq 1$.

Figure 4.6 shows the profit of Firm 1 when $a = 3$ and $a = 1.8$, respectively. Note that $K = 0$ always gives $\pi_1 = 1/3$ – the profit in the symmetric Cournot game. When $a = 3$, the profit is maximised when $K = 0.855$. In this case the cost of investment is so high that it is not profitable for the incumbent Firm 1 to push its marginal cost down to $m_1 = 1$ and thus making it a monopolist. In this case entry is accommodated (A). The solid curves shows the profit in the

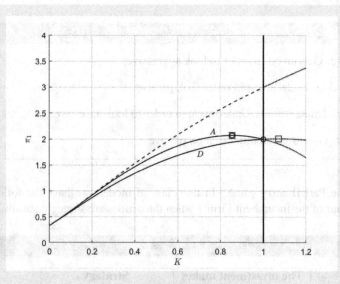

Figure 4.6: Different entry strategies.

two cases $\gamma(K) = K^3$ (upper solid curve A) and $\gamma(K) = K^{1.8}$ (lower solid curve D). The squares denote the maximum values, and the circles the optimal choice of K in each case. The dashed line is the profit without considering the cost $\gamma(K)$, which is included for reference.

When $a = 1.8$, on the other hand, the cost of investing is so low that it is optimal for the incumbent firm to become a monopolist, and hence stop Firm 2 from entering the market. In this case entry is deterred. We note that, just as expected, when the strategic variables are strategic substitutes (recall that this is the case when the reaction curves are downward sloping) and the investment makes the incumbent firm tough, the incumbent should use the Top dog strategy of investing agressively, both in order to accommodate and to deter entry. In this specific model, one can show that

$$\pi_1'(1) = 2 - a.$$

Hence, when $1 \le a \le 2$, the slope of the profit function at $K = 1$ is greater than or equal to 0, so we are in the case shown as the curve D in Figure 4.6 (the maximum of the profit function is at or to the right of $K = 1$). When $a > 2$, the slope at $K = 1$ is negative, so we are in the case described by curve A in Figure 4.6 (the maximum of the profit function is to the left of $K = 1$). The optimal behaviour of the incumbent firm can be summarised as follows:

- When $1 \le a \le 2$: Invest $K = 1$. In this case entry is deterred.

- When $a > 2$: Invest $K < 1$. In this case entry is accommodated.

4.2.4   Taxonomy of strategies

Depending of whether the investment makes the incumbent Firm 1 soft or tough, and whether the firms compete using strategic complements or substitutes, will result in different behaviour of Firm 1. The naming in this taxonomy may seem strange, but is now standard in the information economics literature.

Overview: Market entry strategies

- *Top dog*. Overinvest in order to look aggressive.

- *Puppy dog*. Underinvest in order look passive.

- *Lean and hungry look*. Underinvest in order to look agressive.

- *Fat cat*. Overinvest in order to look passive.

Now consider the Part II entry game. In this class of models we have the following optimal strategic behaviour of the incumbent Firm 1 when the actions are strategic substitutes.

For strategic substitutes

The investment makes the incument firm	Strategy
Tough	Top dog
Soft	Lean and hungry look

We do not prove this result, and refer the interested reader to Section 8.3 in Tirole [50] for a more extensive treatment. When the actions are strategic complements, the strategies of the incumbent firm is dependent on whether entry can be deterred or has to be accommodated. The situation is described in the following table (again, the reader is referred to Section 8.3 in Tirole [50] for details).

For strategic complements		
The investment makes the incument firm	**Entry can be deterred**	**Strategy**
Tough	Yes	Top dog
Tough	No	Puppy dog
Soft	Yes	Lean and hungry look
Soft	No	Fat cat

4.3 Literature notes

The concept of strategic substitutes and complements goes back to Bulow, Geanakopols & Klemperer [6]. A general reference to the content of this chapter is Tirole [50]. See also the original paper Fudenberg & Tirole [15], where the taxonomy of strategies is defined. Example 4.1.1 is based on a problem in Dixit, Skeath & McAdams [12].

4.4 Exercises

Exercise 4.1 The reaction curves of two firms are given by

$$R_1(a_2) = a_2^2$$
$$R_2(a_1) = \frac{a_1 + 1}{2},$$

where the actions satisfy $a_1, a_2 \geq 0$.

a) Find the equilibrium point for the action of each of the firms.

b) Looking at the slopes of the reaction functions, are the actions a_1 and a_2 strategic substitutes or complements? Motivate your answer.

Exercise 4.2 In an entry game, what is the difference between entry being blockaded, deterred and accommodated?

Exercise 4.3 How does a soft firm differ from a tough firm?

Exercise 4.4 What is common for the strategies Top dog and Fat cat on one hand, and the strategies Puppy dog and Lean and hungry look on the other?

Part III

Organisational perspective

Chapter 5

Models with randomness

In this chapter the concept of randomness and the related key statistic notations are introduced. This is essential to understand why information asymmetry and a lack of transparency can cause conflicts in business relationships. It further explains how tasks and risks should best be allocated to achieve efficient outcomes in a collaboration.

5.1 Introduction

Decision-makers in the real estate industry are confronted with randomness in many situations. Take for example the marketing of a project: If a broker is engaged by the building owner to sell a property, it is initially unclear whether a deal will be closed successfully or not. This depends on many factors: Will the broker call enough potential buyers? Will investors be interested in the project characteristics like location, amenities, etc.? Will the development of the broader economy fuel the investment appetite for real estate? Will the weather be good on the day the decision is made? Note that the answer to some of these questions will depend on the effort and qualification of the agent, while others are completely out of control of him or her. The number of calls for instance is observable and can be increased proactively. In contrast the broker has no realistic chance to influence the impact of general market developments or the decision-maker's mood on the day of the decision. When setting up the contract between a broker and a property owner, this has to be accounted for.

5.2 Randomness

5.2.1 Probabilities and random variables

In many cases, the future outcome is unknown. How likely an outcome is, is represented by the *probability* of the outcome. In a situation where there are n possible outcomes, we assign probabilities $P_1, P_2, \ldots, P_n$ that satisfies

$$P_1, P_2, \ldots, P_n \geq 0 \text{ and } \sum_{k=1}^{n} P_k = 1.$$

Here we can allow for n to be infinite, i.e. $n = \infty$. There can also be a situation where we need to assign probabilities for outcomes that are possible to take a value in an interval I. In this case we use a *(probability) density function* f to assign a probability:

$$\text{The probability of being between } a \text{ and } b = \int_a^b f(x)dx.$$

The density function has the following two properties:

- $f(x) \geq 0$.

- $\int_I f(x)dx = 1$.

The normal distribution

The *normal distribution* has

$$f(x) = \frac{1}{\sqrt{2\pi\sigma^2}} e^{-\frac{(x-\mu)^2}{\sigma^2}},$$

where μ is a constant and σ is a strictly positive constant.

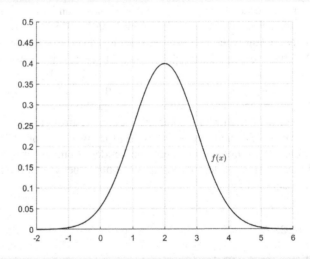

Figure 5.1: Normal density function.

A *random variable* is a variable whose value depends on which outcome occurred. We usually use capital letters to denote random variables (e.g., X, Y or Z). The *expected value* $E(X)$ of the random variable X is a theoretical average value or mean value that we assign to a random variable.

Expected value

The expected value of a random variable is defined by

$$E(X) = \sum_{i=1}^{n} x_i P_i.$$

If we use a model with a density function over an interval I, the expected value is defined as

$$E(X) = \int_I x f(x) dx.$$

For every constant a and b, and every random variable X and Y it holds that

$$E(aX + bY) = aE(X) + bE(Y).$$

Example 5.2.1 Roll a symmetric six-sided die and let X be the number of eyes on the die's top side. Since the die is symmetric we assign the same probability $\frac{1}{6}$ to the event of getting a given number of eyes on the top side. In this case

$$E(X) = 1 \cdot \frac{1}{6} + 2 \cdot \frac{1}{6} + 3 \cdot \frac{1}{6} + 4 \cdot \frac{1}{6} + 5 \cdot \frac{1}{6} + 6 \cdot \frac{1}{6} = \frac{7}{2} = 3.5.$$

Note that in this example the random variable X can take the values 1, 2, 3, 4, 5 or 6, so it is not possible to get the expected value after rolling the die once. This is a typical situation, so the interpretation of the mean as a theoretical average value needs be used with caution. As an example of the mean of a random variable with a density function, if the random variable X has a normal distribution then one can show that

$$E(X) = \mu.$$

To measure the variability of a random variable, we use the *variance* or the *standard deviation*.

Variance and standard deviation

The variance of a random variable is defined as

$$\sigma^2(X) = E\big((X - E(X))^2\big).$$

The standard deviation is the square root of the variance:

$$\sigma(X) = \sqrt{E\big((X - E(X))^2\big)}.$$

For every constant a and b, and every random variable X it holds that

$$\sigma^2(a + bX) = b^2 \sigma^2(X).$$

5.2.2 Preferences over random payoffs

In Chapter 1 we considered preferences defined over different consumption bundles. We are now going to look at preferences over different random payoffs. A random payoff is a random variable representing an in general unknown amount of money that is to be paid out to an individual or firm. As in the case of preferences over consumption bundles, we will use utility functions to represent preferences.

Let X and Y be two random payoffs. Again, we say that a utility function U represents the preference relation $\succeq$ if

$$X \succeq Y \iff U(X) \geq U(Y).$$

If we further can write

$$U(X) = E(u(X))$$

for a function u, then we say that we have an *expected utility representation*. Note that there are two utility functions at play here. If we need to clearly distinguish them, then we call U a *von Neumann-Morgenstern utility function*, and u a *Bernoulli utility function*. The existence of a von Neumann-Morgenstern utility function U does not demand many assumptions, but to guarantee the existence of a Bernoulli utility function u, and thus the existence of an expected utility representation, we need to make quite strong assumptions. From early on, there has been a critique against the assumptions needed to guarantee the existence of an expected utility function. To this day finding alternative axioms which result in different forms of representations of the utility function U are an active field of research. Despite this, we will use the following assumption in the rest of the book.

> **Standing assumption**
>
> We will always assume that the preferences over random payoffs have an expected utility representation such that $u'(x) > 0$.

The condition $u'(x) > 0$ on the Bernoulli utility function means that more is always preferred to less. To calculate $E(u(X))$, we use either

$$\sum_{i=1}^{n} u(x_i) P_i$$

or

$$\int_I u(x) f(x) dx$$

depending on the random variable X.

5.3 Risk

5.3.1 Attitudes towards risk

Given a expected utility representation

$$U(X) = E(u(X)),$$

what can we say about the individual's attitude towards *risk*? First of all, we need to define what we mean with "risk". Let X be a random payoff. "On average" the payoff will be equal to the mean $E(X)$, and we define an individual's attitude towards risk by how the individual ranks X compared with $E(X)$.

- We say that an individual is *risk neutral* if

$$E(u(X)) = u(E(X))$$

for every random payoff X.

- We say that an individual is *risk averse* if

$$E(u(X)) < u(E(X))$$

for every random payoff X.

- We say that an individual is *risk loving* if

$$E(u(X)) > u(E(X))$$

for every random payoff X.

Overview: Risk and utility functions

- A risk-neutral individual has a *linear* utility function $u(x)$.

  Example:

  o $U(x) = x$.

- A risk-averse individual has a *concave* utility function $u(x)$.

  Examples:

  o $u(x) = \sqrt{x}$ for $x \geq 0$,

  o $u(x) = \ln(x + M)$ for $x > -M$, and

  o $u(x) = -e^{-x}$.

- A risk-preferring individual has a *convex* utility function $u(x)$.

  Example:

  o $u(x) = x^2$ for $x \geq 0$.

5.3.2 Coefficient of absolute risk aversion

A quantitative measure of the attitude towards risk is given by the *coefficient of absolute risk aversion* r_A:

$$r_A(x) = -\frac{u''(x)}{u'(x)}.$$

Example 5.3.1 Let
$$u(x) = -e^{-ax}$$
for some $a > 0$. In this case
$$u'(x) = ae^{-ax} \quad \text{and} \quad u''(x) = -a^2 e^{-ax},$$
so
$$r_A(x) = -\frac{u''(x)}{u'(x)} = -\frac{-a^2 e^{-ax}}{ae^{-ax}} = a.$$

5.3.3 Certainty equivalent

An alternative way of measuring the utility of a random payoff X is to calculate its *certainty equivalent*.

Certainty equivalent

A constant CE such that
$$E(u(X)) = u(CE)$$
is called the certainty equivalent of the random payoff X.

One advantage of using the certainty equivalent is that it has the same unit, currency, as the random payoff X.

Example 5.3.2 Let the random payoff X be given by
$$X = \begin{cases} 100 & \text{with probability } 0.25 \\ 10 & \text{with probability } 0.4 \\ -50 & \text{with probability } 0.35. \end{cases}$$

To calculate the certainty equivalent for an individual with utility function
$$u(x) = -e^{-x/100}$$
we start by calculating $E(u(X))$. In this case we get
$$E(u(X)) = -e^{-100/100} \cdot 0.25 - e^{-10/100} \cdot 0.4 - e^{50/100} \cdot 0.35 \approx -1.031.$$

The certainty equivalent CE satisfies
$$-1.031 = -e^{-CE/100} \quad \Leftrightarrow \quad -\frac{c}{100} = \ln 1.031 \quad \Rightarrow \quad CE \approx 3.05.$$

Hence, this individual is indifferent between getting the payoff X and getting the certain amount 3.05.

Example 5.3.3 An individual has utility function

$$u(x) = \sqrt{x}$$

and is offered the random payoff

$$X = \begin{cases} 1 & \text{with probability } 0.5 \\ 9 & \text{with probability } 0.5. \end{cases}$$

The expected value is given by

$$E(X) = 1 \cdot \frac{1}{2} + 9 \cdot \frac{1}{2} = 5,$$

the expected utility by

$$E(u(X)) = \sqrt{1} \cdot \frac{1}{2} + \sqrt{9} \cdot \frac{1}{2} = 2.$$

The certainty equivalent CE is in this case solves the equation

$$2 = \sqrt{CE} \quad \Rightarrow \quad CE = 4.$$

This example is graphically depicted in Figure 5.2.

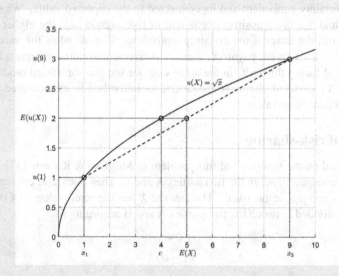

Figure 5.2: Utility function, mean and certainty equivalent.

The connection between the certainty equivalent of a random payoff and the expected value of the same payoff is presented in the following box.

> **Certainty equivalent and expected value**
>
> - An individual/firm is risk neutral $\Leftrightarrow CE = EX$.
>
> - An individual/firm is risk averse $\Leftrightarrow CE < EX$.
>
> - An individual/firm is risk loving $\Leftrightarrow CE > EX$.

Sometimes it is cumbersome to calculate the certainty equivalent. In these cases, the following approximate formula can then be used.

> **An approximation formula for the certainty equivalent**
>
> For a random payoff X it holds that its certainty equivalent satisfies
>
> $$CE \approx E(X) - \frac{r_A(E(X))}{2}\sigma^2(X).$$
>
> If X has a normal distribution and the coefficient of absolute risk aversion is a constant, then this approximation is an equality.

The proof of this can be found in Appendix A.7. This approximation is also useful to get an intuition for the certainty equivalent and its connected to the expected value. We see that for a risk-averse individual, having a positive coefficient of risk aversion r_A, the higher the variance of the random payoff, the lower is the certainty equivalent. That is, when the variance is high, and there is large variation in the payoff X, then a risk-averse individual accepts a low certainty equivalent instead of facing this risk. In the same way, we see that for a fixed random payoff X, i.e. $E(X)$ and $\sigma^2(X)$ are fixed, the more risk-averse an individual is, as measured in higher r_A, the lower is the certainty equivalent.

5.3.4 Optimal risk-sharing

This section is based on the treatment of this problem in Milgrom & Roberts [37]. Let X be an amount that is to be shared between the two parties A and B. They both have constant coefficient of risk aversion ρ_A and ρ_B, respectively. The amount X has expected value $E(X)$ and variance σ^2, and the risk is divided between the two parties A and B according to

$$
\begin{aligned}
X_A &= \alpha X + \gamma \\
X_B &= (1 - \alpha)X - \gamma,
\end{aligned}
$$

where α and γ are two constants. Note that

$$X_A + X_B = X,$$

so the risk X is *shared* between A and B. The certainty equivalent for A and B are given by (using the approximate formula):

$$
\begin{aligned}
CE_A &= E(X_A) - \frac{\rho_A}{2}\sigma^2(X_A) = \alpha E(X) + \gamma - \frac{\rho_A}{2}\alpha^2\sigma^2 \\
CE_B &= E(X_B) - \frac{\rho_B}{2}\sigma^2(X_B) = (1 - \alpha)E(X) - \gamma - \frac{\rho_B}{2}(1 - \alpha)^2\sigma^2.
\end{aligned}
$$

In order to maximise the common welfare of the society, the total certainty equivalent should be maximised. In this case the total certainty equivalent is given by

$$CE_A + CE_B = E(X) - \frac{\sigma^2}{2}\left(\rho_A\alpha^2 + \rho_B(1-\alpha)^2\right) = c(\alpha).$$

The optimal value α satisfies

$$CE'(\alpha) = 0 \iff -\frac{\sigma^2}{2}\left(2\rho_A\alpha - 2\rho_B(1-\alpha)\right) = 0 \implies \alpha = \frac{\rho_B}{\rho_A + \rho_B}.$$

Note that when $\rho_A, \rho_B > 0$ then

$$\alpha = \frac{\rho_B}{\rho_A + \rho_B} \in (0, 1),$$

i.e. it is a fraction of X. Two important special cases are the following:

- When $\rho_A = 0$ and $\rho_B > 0$, then $\alpha = 1$.
- When $\rho_B = 0$ and $\rho_A > 0$, then $\alpha = 0$.

In general, if $\rho_A, \rho_B > 0$ we have

$$\rho_A < \rho_B \iff \alpha > \frac{1}{2}$$

$$\rho_A = \rho_B \iff \alpha = \frac{1}{2}$$

$$\rho_A > \rho_B \iff \alpha < \frac{1}{2}$$

The conclusion is that *the party with the lowest risk aversion takes more of the risk.*

5.4   Risk and uncertainty

When the the payoff X is unknown, but we know the probability of each of the possible values of X, i.e. the situation we have considered so far, then we say that the individual faces *risk*. Consider the random payoff

$$X = \begin{cases} 100 & \text{with probability } 0.5 \\ -100 & \text{with probability } 0.5. \end{cases}$$

In this case

$$E(X) = 0 \quad \text{and} \quad \sigma^2(X) = 10{,}000.$$

But what if the probabilities are not known? Assume that the probability of getting 100 is P, and thus that the probability of getting -100 is $1 - P$. This situation is referred to as *uncertainty* or *ambiguity*. In this case

$$E(X) = 100 \cdot (2p - 1) \quad \text{and} \quad \sigma^2(X) = 20{,}000(1 - p).$$

Now assume that we know that $0.25 \leq P \leq 0.75$. Using this information we see that

$$-50 \leq E(X) \leq 50$$

and
$$5{,}000 \leq E(X) \leq 15{,}000.$$

Hence, even though we do not know the exact value of the probability P, we can at least get a feeling for how the expected value and variance of X behaves. There are also techniques to assign utilities to random payoffs with this property, but this is outside the scope of this book. Finally, we mention the notation of *radical uncertainty*. This is a concept that includes the example of uncertainty above, but more "extreme" examples are also included. In a typical example of radical uncertainty we know neither the probabilities, nor the values the random payoff can have. Understanding how radical uncertainty influences e.g. business decisions is important for investors and banks, as well as for supervising authorities.

5.5 Literature notes

We have only introduced the most basic parts of probability theory and statistics. For a more in-depth description, see e.g. Newbold, Carlson & Thorne [39]. Radical uncertainty is thoroughly discussed in Kay & King [28].

5.6 Exercises

Exercise 5.1 The net random payoff X of a property investment is given by

$$X = \begin{cases} €1{,}000{,}000 & \text{with probability } 0.2 \\ €0 & \text{with probability } 0.5 \\ -€500{,}000 & \text{with probability } 0.3. \end{cases}$$

a) How large is the expected value $E(X)$?

b) How large is the variance $\sigma^2(X)$?

The preferences towards risk of a property investor can be represented by the utility function $u(x) = \ln(x + 800{,}000)$.

c) How large is the expected utility $E(u(X))$?

d) How large is the certainty equivalent CE?

e) Should the investment be done by this property investor?

Exercise 5.2 Let
$$u(x) = \sqrt{x}.$$

Determine the absolute coefficient of risk aversion $r_A(x)$ in this case.

Exercise 5.3 A random payoff has a normal distribution with mean $\mu = 300$ and standard deviation $\sigma = 10$.

a) How large is the certainty equivalent for an investor with constant absolute coefficient of risk aversion $r_A = 2$?

b) How does the size of the certainty equivalent change for a more risk-averse investor?

Exercise 5.4 A firm wants to insure their property, and turns to an insurance company in order to buy an insurance policy. The premium they pay per year is Π and the payout from the insurance during one year is Z. The payoff from this insurance policy for the insurance company is

$$X = Y + \Pi - Z,$$

where the random variable Y represents cash flows from the insurance policies the insurance company already have sold. In order to determine the premium Π of an insurance policy, the insurance company can use their utility function U, and set the premium Π such that

$$E\left[u(Y)\right] = E\left[u(Y + \Pi - Z)\right].$$

The left-hand side is the utility if the policy is not sold to the firm, and the right-hand side is the utility if the policy is sold. Hence, the equation states that the insurance company is indifferent between offering the policy and not offering the policy. This way of setting the premium is called the *zero utility premium principle*, and the premium is referred to as a *zero utility premium*.

To simplify the calculations, we assume that the variability in Y is so low that it can be approximated well with a constant y, i.e. we replace Y with y in the equations above. Show that if the utility function is given by

$$u(x) = -e^{-ax} \quad \text{for a constant } a > 0,$$

then the zero utility premium is

$$\Pi = \frac{1}{a} \ln\left(E\left(e^{aZ}\right)\right).$$

Chapter 6

Contracts

This chapter discusses the role of contracts both in general and in a real estate industry context. It illustrates why and under which conditions different stakeholders collaborate to overcome the limitations of individual firms. It also introduces the various conflict potentials and inefficiencies of such a relationship, namely hidden characteristics and hidden actions. It is an overview chapter, but we will return in detail to many of the topics in later chapters.

6.1   Introduction

Zooming out from individual companies to an ecosystem perspective, the real estate and construction industry is characterised by a very fragmented nature. Due to the complexities of acquiring, developing and operating properties, the tasks are typically split among many different actors (Kahkonen [26]). For instance, in the development of a project, a building owner will commission an architect, engineers, project managers, contractors, etc. The same holds true for the management of properties: Here, among others, the disciplines of fund management, asset management, property management and facility management need to work together to operate buildings smoothly and increase the asset value (McAllister [34]). On top, transaction professionals cover the acquisition and disposal of assets, while specialised consultants are often brought in for brokerage, tax, research or sustainability matters. Exactly which services are performed inhouse or by a third-party actor very much depends on the strategy of the respective investor and/or occupier of an asset, and whether the construction or operational management of real estate are a cost or profit centre to the stakeholder. In consequence, either a primarily vertically integrated model (mostly in-house), a partially vertically disintegrated model (core functions in-house) and a primarily vertically disintegrated model (mostly outsourced) is adopted with the goal to improve operational efficiency and effectiveness (McAllister [34]). Asset owners and occupiers hence rely on an extensive and increasingly diverse network of partners. In many cases, contracts govern these relationships and ensure that the hired agent/outsourcing party acts in accordance with the principal's requirements and best interests in terms of cost, quality and timing of the service.

Figure 6.1 is inspired by Olander & Atkin [40] and gives an idea of the complexity of managing and using a property during its lifecycle and the diverging interests of different project parties.

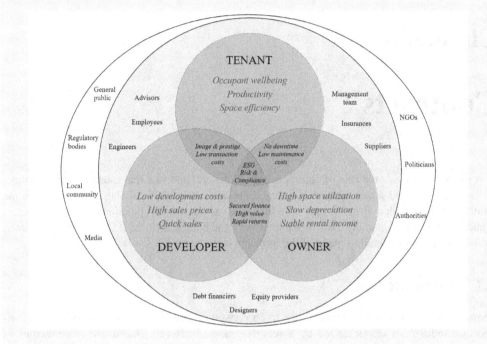

Figure 6.1: Stakeholders in real estate.

6.2 Theory of the firm

In earlier chapters of this book, we have discussed how companies interact in markets driven only by the forces of supply and demand. The classical view of the firm in microeconomics is that of an object using its technology to transform production into products. Recall that the production factors L and K are used in the production, and the quantity q produced is determined by the production function f: $q = f(K, L)$. It is sometimes referred to as looking upon the firm as a "black box", since the transformation from the production factors to the goods is represented exclusively by the production function. Using this model we can understand, e.g., how the cost function can be determined by using the firm's production function. However, that view has taken for granted that the boundaries of companies are given, well-defined properties offering goods or services, and that these offerings are fairly homogeneous (e.g., similar apartments in one building block or standardised services). It also ignores incentives and potential incentive problems as much as organisational aspects.

As long as it is cheaper to direct the flow of goods and services by prices than to negotiate separate contracts for each transaction, markets are the preferred way of interaction. If there is little room for a dispute in a simple, low-value transaction (like buying an apple), there is no need for complex contracts between the party suppling and the party buying a good or service. If the transaction does not yield the expected result for either of the parties, they have no incentives to collaborate again, and will simply engage with other stakeholders for the next transaction.

If the goods or services are not standardised though, companies are needed. From a transaction cost perspective, a firm's boundaries are set so that it is cheaper to do the transaction within the firm than doing the transaction on the market. In other words, the firm's boundaries are defined by efficiency considerations in order to provide incentives.

> "Outside the firm, price movements direct production, which is coordinated through a series of exchange transactions on the market. Within a firm, these market transactions are eliminated and in place of the complicated market structure with exchange transactions is substituted the entrepreneur-coordinator, who directs production." (Coase [8] p. 388.)

Jensen & Meckling [24] see the firm as a legal entity that writes contracts both within the firm as well as with suppliers, customers and other actors with which the firm interacts:

> "The private corporation or firm is simply one form of *legal fiction which serves as a nexus for contracting relationships...*" (Jensen & Meckling [24], p. 311.)

This view is sometimes referred to as the "nexus of contracts" view of the firm.

The theories of the firm presented so far all constribute to a better understanding of the firm and its boundaries, but still can't answer all questions. Oliver Hart argues that the need of defining who has power and control is important (Hart [20]). And it is also for this reason that firms exists:

> "The basic idea is that firms arise in situations where people cannot write good contracts and where allocation of power or control is therefore important." (Hart [20], p. 1.)

With this understanding of the boundary of firm, and the possibilities and limitations of contracts, we are led to study in detail how contracts are constructed and the problems that are inherent when writing contracts.

6.3 Principal-agent relationships

Formally, a contract is a set of rules that regulates how the outcome of an economic situation is to be shared between the parties taking part in it. In many situations in information economics (e.g., in models in contract theory), there is a *principal* and an *agent*. The relationship between the principal and the agent is the following:

- The principal hires the agent to perform a task.

- The principal can observe the outcome of the agent's work.

- The principal can in general not observe the action, or effort, of the agent.

Example 6.3.1 The board of a company hiring a CEO to run the company is one example of a principal-agent relationship. In this case, the contract between them needs to ensure that the actions of the CEO are done in accordance with the wishes of the shareholders, represented by the board, and that the CEO is not acting to maximise his or her own utility.

> **Example 6.3.2** A property developer hiring a contractor is also an example of a principal-agent relationship. In this case, the developer needs to ensure that the contractor builds according to the developer's intentions, but also that the construction is made in time and within the budget agreed upon.

The fact that the principal and the agent in general have different goals (utility functions), and that the principal usually only can observe the outcome, and not the actions of the agent, can lead to a *principal-agent problem*.

In principal-agent models, the principal is often a firm, and the agent could be an employee or a contractorer. Since a firm has many possibilities of handle risk, it is usual to make the following assumptions:

- The agent is risk averse.

- The principal is risk neutral.

Note, however, that there are cases when the opposite attitudes towards risk are more reasonable to assume. One example is when a person, the principal in this case, hires a lawyer, the agent, working at a large law firm. In this case the principal, being an individual, is probably risk averse, while the lawer, working in (and being supported by) a big law firm, can be assumed to be risk neutral.

6.4 Contract types

To govern the relationship between a principal and an agent, contracts are used to regulate the interactions in a formal way (Kadefors & Bröchner [25]). This allows objectives to be aligned and provides incentives for the parties to collaborate over a longer period of time. In this chapter, we will discuss how a contract and in particular the agent's remuneration should be set up to account for the interests of both parties.

In a principal-agent relationship, there are several ways in which the profit of the relationship can be divided. The following are common types of contracts in this situation.

> **Overview: Contract types**
>
> Let π be the profit that is to be shared between the principal and the agent.
>
> - *Fixed-fee contract*: The principal gets a fixed amount F, and the agent gets $\pi - F$, or the principal gets $\pi - F$ and the agent gets F.
>
> - *Piecewise contract*: The agent gets an amount wa proportional to the number of units a the agent produces, and the principal gets $\pi - wa$.
>
> - *Profit sharing contract*: The principal gets the fraction $\gamma\pi$, and the agent gets the fraction $(1 - \gamma)\pi$ for some $0 < \gamma < 1$.

One of the goals in contract theory is to understand in which situations each of these types of contract can be chosen by the principal in order to avoid, if possible, moral hazard as the equilibrium outcome. Typically, we are concerned with two types of variables influencing the profit of the principal-agent relationship: The effort put down by the agent and the way in which randomness plays a part. This in turn results in *effiency in production* and *efficiency in risk bearing*. Effiency in production means that the effort put down by the agent is the one that maximises the total profit, and efficiency in risk bearing means that the risks are borne in relation to the risk aversion of the principal and agent respectively.

6.5 Complete and incomplete contracts

In general it is not possible to write contracts based on the effort of an agent, the reason being that it is typically hard to observe the effort put down by the agent. In classifying contracts based on characteristics of the parts of the contractual agreement, the following two properties are important.

Properties of actions

- *Observable*: An action is observable if it is possible for both the principal and the agent to observe the action.

- *Verifiable*: An action is verifiable if it is possible to get the action verified by a third party, e.g., by a court of law.

There are some economists who are critical of the distinction between observable and verifiable. Lind & Nyström [33] argue that if something is observable but not verifiable ex post (after the contract has been signed), then the parties writing the contract can agree ex ante (before the contract has been signed) to make it is possible to verify the outcome. We will, however, keep the distinction, as it is a good way of understanding the difference between complete and incomplete contracts. For more on the critique, see the paper Lind & Nyström [33] and references therein.

Using what is observable and what is verifiable, we arrive at the following classification of contracts:

Classification of contracts

Contract	Is everything observable to everyone?	Is the observable information also verifiable?
Complete contingent	Yes	Yes
Complete	No	Yes
Incomplete	No	No

In contracts, the following are usually assumed:

- Quantity is observable and verifiable.

- Quality is observable but not verifiable.

- Effort is neither observable nor verifiable.

It is often difficult to define all possible requirements from all parties up front. For instance, a brokerage agreement for a long-term lead mandate consists of only a few formal terms such as fees, duration and reporting structures, while many detailed duties and obligations are not written down. Due to their inability to account for unforeseen circumstances and details, formal contracts are "incomplete" by nature. Instead, they rely on trust and the mutual dependency of the parties entering into them. The contract stays in force mostly because its breakdown would hurt all parties. The same is true for the example of a property lease. A corporate tenant evicted from its premises will hardly find a building with similar features quickly. Equally, if a tenant was to move out at short notice, the landlord will struggle to find a new tenant without any vacancy periods. Thus, each could threaten the other in pursuit of a better rent. In a long-term contract that specifies the rent, tenure and use of the property, both parties benefit.

Example 6.5.1 A property manager is hiring a broker to find tenants to a commerical real estate building. The number of offices that are brokered during a month is denoted q, and is a function of the effort e the broker puts down trying to find tenants. There is, however, also randomness involved in the process of effort being transferred into the number of contracts being brokered. In this example we assume that

$$q = e + X,$$

where X is a random variable. This random variable is assumed to have mean $E(X) = 0$ and variance $\sigma^2(X) = v$. The fact that $E(X) = 0$ implies that

$$E(q) = E(e + X) = e + E(X) = e,$$

so, "on average", the number of offices that are brokered during a month is equal to the effort put down by the broker. On the other hand, if the variance is high, then the observed q can deviate highly from the effort e put down by the broker. Let us now consider the types of contract that can be written depending on the situation at hand.

- If $\sigma^2(X) = 0$, then there is no randomness, and we have $q = e$. Hence, in this case both effort and quantity are observable and verifiable, so we can write complete contingent contracts in this case.

- If $\sigma^2(X) > 0$, then there is randomness and there are two cases to consider.

  o If q is observable and verifiable, while e is only observable by the agent and not verifiable, then we are in the situation defining a complete contract: Not everything is verifiable (in this case the effort e), while what is observable (in this case the number q of offices that are brokered during a month) is also verifiable.

○ If the number of offices that are brokered during a month is reported by the agent, then the agent might lie to the principal, and not even the number q of offices that are brokered during a month is verifiable. In this case only incomplete contracts are possible to write.

6.6 Asymmetric information and opportunistic behaviour

In an ecosystem as described in Section 6.1, both sides (an asset owner as "principal" and the respective partners as "agents") benefit from entering into collaborations. Nevertheless, it frequently occurs that one party has information that the other party lacks. This is known as *information asymmetry*. In this book we focus on two situations of asymmetric information: *Hidden characteristics* and *hidden actions*. Hidden characteristics appear before the contract is signed, or ex ante, and will be studied in detail in Chapter 7, while hidden actions appear after the contract is signed, or ex post, and is the topic of Chapter 8.

While the mere existence of information asymmetry is not a problem, diverging risk profiles and potential economic advantages may motivate one of the actors to exploit the set-up and put their own interests above the shared goals. This is known as *opportunistic behaviour*. In summary, for challenges to arise between two contract parties, the following conditions have to be fulfilled:

> **Conditions for opportunistic behaviour**
>
> • Availability of a profit (or, more generally, a surplus of some kind).
>
> • The presence of an information asymmetry.
>
> • A conflict of interest.

Problems resulting from this are economic disadvantages for the other party, an inefficient use of resources and in consequence a loss of welfare (Schieg [46]). For instance, in the absence of constant performance monitoring and effective incentive structures, a local service provider (e.g., a facility manager or broker) to a real estate investor may choose to reduce the efforts to maximise its own operational profit, even if this may be contrary to the objective of a well-maintained respectively fully let building. We will see in the following sections, why such behaviour is difficult to avoid entirely but how it can be mitigated by means of well-structured contracts. Depending on whether the asymmetric information is based on hidden characteristics or hidden actions, opportunistic behaviour can lead to an equilibrium with *adverse selection* or *moral hazard* respectively.

> **Overview: Equilibria from opportunistic behaviour**
>
> | Property | Possible equilibrium |
> |---|---|
> | Hidden characteristic | Adverse selection |
> | Hidden action | Moral hazard |

Specific challenges arising from information asymmetry before and after agreeing to a contract will be explored in more detail in Chapters 7 and 8 respectively.

6.7 Literature notes

For more on the topics in the chapter, see e.g. Hendrikse [22], from which the table "Classification of contracts" is taken, or Bolton & Dewatripont [5]. Hart [19] provides a non-technical overview of the theory of the firm from an economic prespective aimed at lawyers and others in the legal profession. Also see the references referred to in the text.

6.8 Exercises

Exercise 6.1 What is the difference between a complete and an incomplete contract?

Exercise 6.2 What is missing in the description of a firm consisting of many principal-agent relationships?

Exercise 6.3 Why is the existence of incomplete contracts an explanation of the boundary of the firm?

Chapter 7

Hidden characteristics and adverse selection

This chapter focuses on hidden characteristics, the resulting inefficiencies and potential ways to mitigate them before agreeing to a contract. We distinguish between two scenarios: hidden characteristics in principal-agent relationships (such as selection of service providers or employee recruitment) and hidden characteristics in other contractual relationships (e.g., lease agreements, property insurances and asset transactions).

7.1   Introduction

Transparency is key to the efficient operation of markets. As in many other sectors, this is also true for the real estate and construction industry. To compete against other, more transparent asset classes such as stocks or bonds in the allocation of investments, and understand the industry's impact on the environment and communities, the pressure to improve transparency is growing. Relevant areas include e.g., performance measurement, market data, governance of listed vehicles, regulatory and legal frameworks, transaction processes and sustainability.[1] While individual actors may benefit from the absence of transparency in any of these fields, the resulting equilibrium is inefficient from an overall perspective. Contracts that account for situations of asymmetric information, be it in asset transactions, recruitment or service provider engagements, can help reduce these inefficiencies. We will start with the selection process before agreeing to a contract in this chapter. The issue of intransparency during the contractual relationship will be discussed in Chapter 8. Before moving on to examples, we recall the following facts from Chapter 6.

Hidden characteristics and adverse selection	
Property	**Possible equilibrium**
Hidden characteristic	Adverse selection
Hidden characteristics appear before the contract is signed, or ex ante.	

---

[1]https://www.jll.co.uk/en/trends-and-insights/research/global-real-estate-transparency-index

As a first example, let us consider the case of service provider selection. Given a number of potential candidates, an investor or asset manager will perform a screening of their main characteristics to identify the most promising options. To get a more detailed picture of each company, financial information like annual reports provide an initial idea of the company's standing. In addition, market reports (third-party information) summarise the perception of the industry and offer benchmarks. However, e.g., the motivation and suitability of the key contacts of a company for the mandate in question can hardly be derived from such resources. Here, pitches, references and case studies can support the pre-signing selection process and offer candidates an opportunity for proactive signalling.

As a second example, let us consider the transaction process of an asset. To the buyer, factors like the maintenance level or the status of the building systems are not known at the beginning of an acquisition. While the status is only known to the seller, it is not publicly observable, which in turn makes it difficult for buyers to identify potential risks and price them adequately. There are of course disclosure agreements in sales purchase agreements (SPA) that require sellers to reveal information about an asset. Nevertheless, full transparency is not entirely enforceable in practice due to difficulty of proving buyer's claims (asymmetric information). In consequence, buyers have no choice but to judge by appearance of an asset. Anticipating this condition, sellers in some cases perform fake improvements to achieve higher sales prices (Ben-Shahar [4]).

- Shortly before listing, maintenance efforts are increased by owners as a signalling mechanism for better quality and verifiable improvements (e.g., investment in equipment, renovation of walls, gardening, ...).

- Depending on the building maintenance level (good or bad), signalling costs, and signalling rewards, owners may choose different strategies and the strategies may lead to an inefficient outcome from a welfare perspective.

- If full information was available (i.e., the maintenance level is publicly observable), a pre-transaction maintenance investment would only be made if it was fully reflected in the post-investment transaction price (i.e., marginal cost < marginal benefit).

- If a false investment in asset improvements is feasible and indistinguishable to prospective buyers from a real investment, and improvements are efficiently incorporated into prices, then there is a unique equilibrium in which owners will fake an investment in asset improvements in both well- and poorly maintained assets. These fake improvements will lead to a waste of resources since the building is improved only superficially.

After listing and during the acquisition process, due diligence investigations (for technical, financial, legal, ... matters) are one way for the potential buyer to reduce information asymmetry

7.2 Separating and pooling equilibria

There are two types of equilibria that we have to distinguish between when considering possible equilibria when there are hidden characteristics.

- A *pooling equilibrium* is an equilibrium in which different types are not differentiated in equilibrium.

- A *separating equilibrium* is an equilibrium in which different types are differentiated in equilibrium.

In a pooling equilibrium, everyone being offered a contract, and accepting it, will choose the same action. If we end up in an equilibrium with adverse selection, then this is a pooling equilibrium. If we, on the other hand, end up in a separating equilibrium, then the ones being offered a contract, and choosing to accept it, will choose actions depending on their characteristics.

7.3 Hidden characteristics and adverse selection

Assume that there is a number of small rental properties for sale, and that the level of quality of a property can either be good or bad, as measured by the maintenance the current owner has carried out. Since it is possible for the seller to make minor last-minute maintenance to make the property look better than it is, if the buyer does not have the information about the quality of the property, then it is not possible for an uninformed buyer to distinguish between a property with a high and low level of maintenance. Consider the following case: An owner of a badly maintained property is prepared to sell it for 200 (in millions of euros), and an owner of well-maintained property is prepared to sell it for 500 (in millions of euros). There are 10 badly maintained properties and 10 well-maintained properties. There are many buyers, and they are prepared to pay 300 (in millions of euros) for a badly maintained property, and pay 600 (in millions of euros) for a well-maintained property. We summarise the situation in Table 7.1.

Table 7.1: The number of sellers and the buyers, and their prices.

	Properties with bad maintenance	Properties with good maintenance
Buyers' price	300	600
Sellers' price	200	500

We will look at the following three cases:

Three different information situations

A. Both buyers and sellers have full information regarding the quality of the property.

B. Neither the buyers nor the sellers have full information regarding the quality of the property.

C. The sellers, but not the buyers, have knowledge regarding the quality of their respective properties.

A. All sellers and buyers have full information

Looking first at the case of badly maintained properties, we see that the price the buyers are prepared to pay (300), is higher than the price the sellers accept (200). This means that all real estate assets will be sold – but at which price? The price will be 300, and the reason is the following. Since there are many potential buyers, all of them valuing a bad real estate asset to 300, if any buyer would try to buy an asset for an amount less of 300, the seller will reject it because he or she knows that there will come along another buyer prepared to pay 300. Since no buyer will pay more than the 300 it values a bad real estate asset at, the price will be exactly 300.

In this case supply meets demand for badly maintained properties when the price is 300, and at this price 10 real estate assets are sold. In the same manner, supply meets demand in the market for good real estate assets when the price is equal to 600, and the quantity sold is again 10.

B. Neither the sellers nor the buyers have full information

This is also a case of symmetric information. We assume that both the buyers and the sellers are risk-neutral. This means (see Section 5.3.1) that both buyers and sellers value a random payoff by its expected value. Since there are 10 real estate assets that are good and bad respectively, the probability of getting a good asset is

$$\frac{10}{10 + 10} = \frac{1}{2}.$$

In the same way, the probability of getting a bad asset is

$$\frac{10}{10 + 10} = \frac{1}{2}.$$

This results in the following expected values for the buyers and the sellers:

$$\text{Expected value of a property for the buyers} \quad = \quad 300 \cdot \frac{1}{2} + 600 \cdot \frac{1}{2} = 450.$$

$$\text{Expected value of a property for the sellers} \quad = \quad 200 \cdot \frac{1}{2} + 500 \cdot \frac{1}{2} = 350.$$

Here we see that the supply meets the demand at the price 450, and at this price every property is sold. This means that, again, all the 20 properties are sold; in this case for the price 450 each. What happens in this case is that the 10 buyers that are lucky enough to get a good property only have to pay 450 for a good property they value to 600, while the buyers of a bad real estate asset have to pay 450 for a property they value to 300.

C. The sellers have full information, and the buyers have no information

Now assume that the sellers know the quality of their property, but that the buyers have no information about the maintenance quality. The buyers are still assumed to be risk-neutral, so they are willing to pay 450 for a property of unknown quality. This is known by the sellers, especially by the sellers of well-maintained properties. They realise that a buyer cannot distinguish between a good and a badly maintained property, so no buyer will pay more than 450 for any of the properties. The conclusion is that owners of a well-maintained property will withdraw their properties from the market, and only the badly maintained properties will remain. This is, in turn, also realised by the buyers, so they will know that the only assets on the market are the bad ones. Hence, only the badly maintained properties, that are valued by the sellers at 200 are sold, and for the price 300. The well-maintained properties will remain unsold, so only the 10 bad real estate assets will be sold. It follows that in the resulting equilibrium *the low-quality badly maintained properties drive the well-maintained properties out of the market*, i.e. we end up in an equilibrium with *adverse selection*.

Final remarks

If we end up with adverse selection in equilibrium in case C with asymmetric information will crucially depend on the following two parameters:

- The reservation prices.

- The proportion of badly maintained properties in the market.

How the proportion of badly maintained properties influences the asymmetric information case is studied in Exercise 7.2.

This example is a version of the "market for lemons" example described in Akerlof [1]. A "lemon" is a car that is of low quality, but this lower quality is not possible to detect by only checking the car and taking it for a test drive. Instead this will reveal itself, say, a couple of weeks after a lemon has been bought.

7.4 Methods to avoid adverse selection

There are several ways in which it is possible to avoid ending up in an equilibrium with adverse selection. The main difference between them is who it is in the contractual situation that is instigating the transfer of information.

- *Screening*: The uninformed party seeks information from the informed party.

- *Signalling*: The informed party wants to convey information to the uninformed party.

In the following sections we will give several examples of situations in which screening and signalling are feasible selection methods. In addition, third-party information can be referred to. This means that an organisation that is not one of the two parties in a transaction helps to force the parties to share information, thereby decreasing the information asymmetry.

7.4.1 Screening

A general tool

In the case of screening, the uninformed party seeks information from the informed party. We use the following general set-up as a tool to analyse situations where we use screening to avoid adverse selection.

> **Good and bad in contracts**
>
> A contract consists of offering a customer or employee pairs (B, G), where B is an amount of a *bad* and G is an amount of a *good* (from the customer's or employee's perspective).

A bad is something an individual wants less of, and a good is something an individual wants more of, and the idea of using a bad and a good is to construct a cleverly chosen *menu of contracts*. If this is possible, then *self-selection* will lead to a separating equilibrium, and adverse selection is avoided.

Consider a coordinate system where the level of the bad is on the x-axis, and the level of the good is on the y-axis. This means that utility increases as we move in the north-west direction (see Figure 7.1). A low risk customer/employee will have *flat* indifference curves, while a high risk customer/employee will have *steep* indifference curves. These features make it possible to create a menu of contracts that separates high and low risk customers. To understand the difference in the indifference curves, consider a high risk individual. Since an indifference curve represents the combinations of the good and the bad that has *the same utility*, it is reasonable to assume that as the amount of bad increases for a high risk individual, the amount of good needs to increase with a relatively large amount to compensate for the increase in the bad. For a low risk individual, the amount of good along an indifference curve also needs to increase as the amount of the bad increases, but this compensation will not be as high as for a high risk customer. Thus, we see steep indifference curves for high risk individuals, and flat indifference curves for low risk customers.

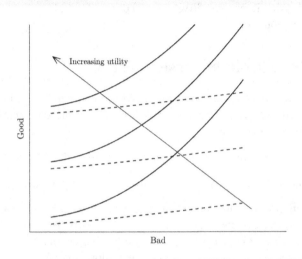

Figure 7.1: Indifference curves of high and low risk actors.

As an example of the general set-up, consider an insurance company that is offering property insurance. The customers are either high risk or low risk customers. There is a risk of getting an equilibrium with adverse selection (only high risk customers buy insurance). This means that the insurance company will not be able to sell insurance to low risk property owners, i.e. they miss out on a large portion of the potential customer base. In order to also attract low risk customers, the company must be able to distinguish high risk from low risk customers. In this example we let

$$(B, G) = (\text{Deductible}, \text{Premium reduction}).$$

The "trick" here is to introduce *two* different insurance policies: One high-deductable policy with a high premium reduction, and one low-deductible policy with a low premium reduction. We now claim the following:

> **Insurance contracts devised to avoid adverse selection**
>
> With this menu of contracts, the low risk customers want to sign up for a high-deductible policy (with a high premium reduction), while the high risk customers want to sign up for a low-deductible coverage policy (with a low premium reduction).

We see depicted in Figure 7.2 the two contracts, Contract I, with a low deductible and a low premium reduction, and Contract II, with a high deductible and a high premium reduction.

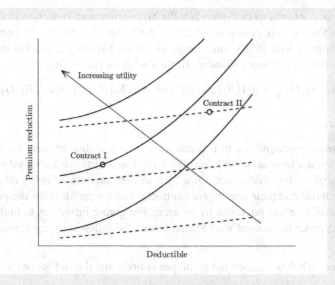

Figure 7.2: Indifference curves with a menu of contracts.

By using the facts that low risk customers have flat indifference curves, and high risk customers have steep indifference curves, we see that Contract II is preferred by low risk customers, and Contract I is preferred by high risk customers. It is important to define the two contracts in such a way so that the resulting equlibrium really is a separating equilibrium. In Figure 7.3, an example of a menu of contracts which results in a pooling equilibrium is given.

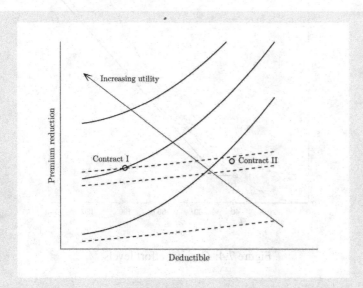

Figure 7.3: Menu of contracts with a pooling equilibrium.

With the menu of contracts as in Figure 7.3, the higher premium reduction in Contract II is not high enough for the low risk customers to accept the higher deductible. In formulas, if we want Group 1 of customers with utility function u_1 to choose Contract I, and Group 2 of customers with utility function u_2 to choose Contract II, then we must ensure that

$$u_1\big((B_I, G_I)\big) > u_1\big((B_{II}, G_{II})\big) \quad \text{and} \quad u_2\big((B_{II}, G_{II})\big) > u_2\big((B_I, G_I)\big).$$

Salary structures

In order to increase production, a firm wants to give high-ability workers an incentive to work hard by giving them a high salary, while still paying low-ability workers a salary. In this model the output is equal to the effort e put down by a worker, and this effort is observable. Hence, it is possible to write complete contingent contracts, and the problem for the principal is not in observing the level of effort put down by an agent, but giving incentives to high-ability workers to work hard. In order to succeed with this ambition, the following wage scheme is used by the firm:

- If the effort is below e_0, then the employee is fired, and doesn't get any salary: $w(e) = 0$

- If the effort is between e_0 and e^*, then the salary is w_0: $w(e) = w_0$

- If the effort is above e^*, then the salary increases linearly:

$$w(e) = w_0 + b(e - e^*),$$

where $b > 0$ is a constant.

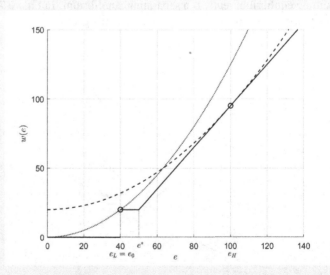

Figure 7.4: Optimal effort levels.

This scheme is depicted as the solid lines in Figure 7.4. In this model we have, using the notation from the general tool,

$$(B, G) = (e, w(e)).$$

> **The optimal behaviour of the employees**
>
> - A low-ability worker has steep indifference curves and will put down the effort $e_L = e_0$ and get the salary w_0.
>
> - A high-ability worker has flat indifference curves and will put down the effort $e_H > e^*$ and get the salary $w_0 + b(e_h - e^*)$.

By using screening, the employer is able to arrive at a separating equilibrium where the low-ability workers put down the effort e_0, and the high-ability workers put down an effort that is strictly larger than e^*. The separating equilibrium is depicted in Figure 7.4. Here, the chosen effort level for a low-ability worker is represented by the left circle, and the chosen effort level for a high-ability worker is represented by the right circle.

Screening when hiring

A typical situation when sceening is used is when a firm is hiring a new employee. In order to find out if a candidate for a position is suitable, the principal needs to meet the agent (usually several times).

> **Examples of screening when hiring**
>
> - *Interviews*, in which the principal meets the agent in order to try to find out which characteristics the agent has.
>
> - *Tests*, which are used to find out the agent's level of knowledge in general or within a certain area.

7.4.2 Signalling

Signalling means that the informed party wants to convey information to the uninformed party. A *signal* is something that informs an uninformed party, e.g., a principal, about the characteristic of the informed party, e.g., an agent.

Signalling when setting the salary

Consider a firm having a lot of employees. Among the employees there are two types of workers: high-ability workers and low-ability workers. A high-ability worker has the capability of working harder than a low-ability worker, and the employer wants to reward high-ability workers by giving them a higher salary. If an employee is known to be a high-ability worker, then the salary is w_H, and if an employee is known to be a low-ability worker, then the salary is w_L. Here it is assumed that $w_L < w_H$. Hence, the full information solution, i.e. when the type of each employee is known, then the employer gives a high-ability worker the salary w_H, and a low-ability worker the salary w_L.

The problem for the employer is that it is impossible (or at least very hard) to distinguish between high- and low-ability workers by just observning them, so the full information solution described above is not possible to implement. Due to this fact, the high-ability workers want to

112

show the employer that they have a high ability. Of the employed, the fraction $0 \le \alpha \le 1$ are high-ability workers, and hence the fraction $1 - \alpha$ are low-ability workers. If the employer cannot distinguish between high- and low-ability workers, then every worker will get the same wage, and in this case the resulting equilibrium is a pooling equilibrium. If there is a pooling equilibrium, then every employee is paid w.

Now assume that there is a possibility for the high-ability workers to show to the employer that they have a high ability. In our examples we let this be done by the high-ability workers participating in some form of education. In a classical signalling situation, the education is only a way of signalling – it will not increase the output from a high-ability worker (but in some cases the signal will actually be beneficial for the production). We will consider two different models of signalling. First we consider the model by Spence [47], and then the model by Stiglitz [48].

The Spence model

In Spence's model, each employee chooses the level of education he or she wants to reach. The cost for a low-ability worker to reach level y of education is $c_L \cdot y$, and for a high-ability worker it is $c_H \cdot y$, where $c_L > c_H$. Hence, it is more expensive for a low-ability worker to reach education level y than it is for a high-ability worker. In order for the signalling to work, the employer needs to be able to distinguish between the two groups of employees, thus reaching a separating equilibrium. Assume that the employer uses the following wage scheme defined in terms of the level of education:

$$w(y) = \begin{cases} w_L & \text{if } y < y^* \\ w_H & \text{if } y \ge y^*. \end{cases}$$

With this type of wage scheme, every employee will choose either $y = 0$ or $y = y^*$; see Figure

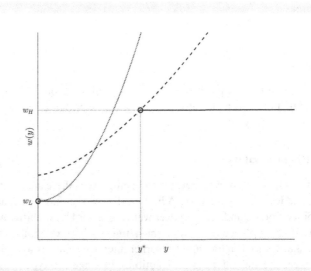

Figure 7.5: Optimal education levels.

7.5. The employer wants the high-ability workers to choose $y = y^*$, and the low-ability workers to choose $y = 0$. In order for this to be optimal for the two groups, the level y^* needs to satisfy

$$w_L - c_L y^* \leq 0 \text{ (the low-ability workers should not choose } y^*)$$

and

$$w_H - c_H y^* \geq 0 \text{ (the high-ability workers should choose } y^*).$$

These two conditions results in the following inequalities for y^*:

$$\frac{w_L}{c_L} \leq y^* \leq \frac{w_H}{c_H}. \tag{7.1}$$

Since $w_L < w_H$ and $c_L > c_H$, it will always hold that

$$\frac{w_L}{c_L} < \frac{w_H}{c_H}.$$

This means that there in fact will exist infinitely many choices of y^* that satisfy Equation (7.1), i.e. such that signalling results in a separating equilibrium.

Note the difference between this model and Lazear's model in Section 7.4.1. In Lazear's model the employee chooses the level of effort to put down, and this effort level will influence the output of the firm. In Spence's model, the level of education is a signal: It does not influence the output of the firm, but only serves to reveal the type (high-ability or low-ability) of an employee.

The Stiglitz model

In Stiglitz's model of signalling, the cost of the education is a constant C, and it is only possible for a high-ability worker to get the education; low-ability workers have no choice of participating in the education. Of the workers, the fraction α are high-ability workers. In an equilibrium no one wants to change their decision, and in this model the only choice are for a high-ability worker to choose to get the education or not. Hence, in an equilibrium no high-ability worker wants to change his or her decision of getting the education or not.

In a separating equilibrium high-ability workers choose to be educated. If a high-ability worker does not participate in the education, then he or she will be assumed to have low ability, and get paid the salary of a low-ability worker. In order for it to be profitable for the high-ability workers to participate in the education it must hold that

$$w_H - C > w_L \iff w_H - w_L > C.$$

Hence, if this condition holds, a separating equilibrium is feasible. In a pooling equilibrium, everyone is paid the same salary w, which is defined as the average salary taking into account the fraction of high-ability workers among the employees:

$$\overline{w} = \alpha w_H + (1 - \alpha) w_L.$$

If

$$w_H - C < \overline{w} \iff w_H - \overline{w} < C,$$

then it is not beneficial for a high-ability worker to get education. Hence, in this case a pooling equilibrium is feasible.

We conclude that the possible equilibria depend on the values of the parameters α and C. Furthermore, for some values of the the parameters α and C, it is possible to have *both* a pooling or a separating equilibrium. How can this be possible?

- If *all* high-ability workers choose to educate, then it is not optimal for a given high-ability worker to skip the education, i.e. to deviate.

- If *no* high-ability worker chooses to educate, then it is not optimal for a given worker to get the education, i.e. to deviate.

Which one of the two equilibria that will be chosen is not possible to determine. The only thing we know is that given that the parameters satisfies the conditions

$$C < w_H - w_L \text{ and } w_H - w_L < \frac{C}{1-\alpha},$$

if *all* high-ability workers choose to educate, then no high-ability worker has incentives not to take the education, and if *no* high-ability worker chooses to educate, then no high-ability worker has incentives to participate in the education. See Appendix A.8 for more on the mathematics of the Stiglitz model.

7.5 Literature notes

For a general introduction to hidden characteristics and adverse selection, see Perloff [43], Varian [53] or Hendrikse [22]. The seminal paper on "lemons" is Akerlof [1], and the model described in Section 7.1 is inspired by the one used in Ben-Shahar [4] (although the model in that paper is used to explain a type of signalling). The model described in Section 7.4.1 has been studied in Lazear [31], and the orignal papers on signalling are Spence [47] and Stiglitz [48]. The section on the Stiglitz model is based on the presentation in Perloff [43].

7.6 Exercises

Exercise 7.1 What is the difference, from an information perspective, between screening and signalling?

Exercise 7.2 Consider the "market for lemons" as described in Section 7.3, with the difference that the proportion of badly maintained properties is $\alpha \in [0, 1]$. For which values of α will there not be adverse selection in equilibrium?

Exercise 7.3 A real estate company has two types of employees: High-ability workers and low-ability workers. The high-ability workers deliver a high output, and the low-ability workers deliver a low output. In order to screen them, the firm offers their workers the following two different wage schemes.

	Wage during year 1	Wage from year 2 and onwards
Wage scheme I	w	w
Wage scheme II	w_H	w_L or w_H

Hence, choosing wage scheme I, the employee gets the wage w every year until he or she ends their employment or retires. In contrast, wage scheme II has a wage revision after one year. The first year the wage is $w_H > w$. If the employee after one year delivers a high level of output, then the wage is w_H every year until he or she ends their employment or retires. If, on the other hand, the employee delivers a low level of output, then the wage is $w_L < w$ every year until he or she ends their employment or retires. The total wage for an employee is

$$\sum_{t=1}^{T} w(t),$$

where T is the time until an employee leaves the company, and $w(t)$ is the wage in year t.

a) If the time until an employee leaves the company is $T = 10$ years for all employees (in practice, we can consider this as the average time an employee stays employed), write down the conditions we must demand of w_L, w and w_M in order for it not to be profitable for the low-ability workers to choose wage scheme II.

b) Assume that $w_L = 0.9$, $w = 1$ and $w_H = 2$. What will the probable outcome be for the real estate company?

Exercise 7.4 Two groups of customers wanting to rent an apartment have utility functions

$$u_1(L, R) = L - 2R^2$$

and

$$u_2(L, R) = 3L - 6R^3,$$

where L is the level of renovation, and R is the rent.

a) Which of the utility functions represents the group of customers preferring a low rent to a renovated apartment?

b) In order to screen the two groups, the landlord introduces two different rent contracts:

	Level of renovation L	Rent R (in €1,000)
Contract I	2	1
Contract II	4	2

Show that the resulting equilibrium is a pooling one, i.e. there is no screening in this case. What could be the result of this equilibrium?

c) The landlord realises the inefficiency of the rent contract described in b), and instead introduces the following contracts:

	Level of renovation L	Rent R (in €1,000)
Contract I	2	1
Contract II	5	1.5

Show that the resulting equilibrium is a separating one.

Chapter 8

Hidden actions and moral hazard

In this chapter we address a number of challenges after agreeing to a contract, such as how to avoid moral hazard and incentivise the parties to perform to their best ability. Various ways of dealing with these risks are explained and illustrated in the context of property valuation, construction, and facility management.

8.1   Introduction

The typical situation studied in academic contract theory is the principal-agent situation. In the paper "The theory of contracts" by Hart & Holmström [21], they explicitly write that "...throughout we will restrict attention to cases in which informational asymmetries arise only subsequent to contracting" (Hart & Holmström [21], p. 74), i.e. they only consider hidden actions and moral hazard. Although understanding how to write contracts when there are hidden characteristics is important, the ways of using screening or signalling to avoid ending up in an equilibrium where there is adverse selction is fairly straightforward to analyse. If we have created a contract that results in a separating equilibrium, then all is usually fine. Writing contracts when there is a hidden action is, on the other hand, harder. As we will see, there are two important agents contraints that the principal has to take into consideration when creating a contract, and even in simple models, the calculations become quite involved. Again, we remind the reader of the following summary of hidden actions and moral hazard from Chapter 6.

Hidden actions and moral hazard	
Property	**Possible equilibrium**
Hidden action	Moral hazard

Hidden actions appear after the contract is signed, or ex post.

8.2   Motivation in principal-agent relationships

One example of the timeline of a contractual situation is described in Figure 8.1. We see that, as it is depicted there, the result of a contracting situation is a Stackelberg type of game, i.e. it is a "leader-follower" situation. As in the Stackelberg models considered in Chapter 3 on oligopolies, the way we solve it, and other sequential games, is by starting at the end. In the case of a principal-agent situation, this means that we start with the agent. For a principal offering an agent a contract, there are in general two problems:

1) The agent can refuse to accept the contract.

2) The agent accepts the contract, but chooses a level of effort that is suboptimal from the principal's point of view.

From an incentive perspective, a contract between a principal and agent has to satisfy the following two constraints.

> ### Constraints in contract design
>
> - The *participation constraint*: The agent must get at least as high utility as he or she can get by not accepting the contract (e.g., by getting to work somewhere else).
>
> - The *incentive compatibility constraint*: The agent uses the effort that maximises his or her utility.

In practice, this means that the principal has to take these two constraints into account when constructing a contract to offer to an agent. The participation coinstraint is the same thing as an agent having an "outside option", i.e. the opportunity of going somewhere else to work or find a contractor. On the other hand, the incentive compatibility constraint means that the principal, when offering a contract, must take into account the fact that the agent will choose the action that maximises his or her utility.

8.3 Models with hidden actions

The following general modelling approach to principal-agent situations is taken from Hart & Holmström [21]. An agent puts down the effort e. Depending on the effort, there is a random payoff $Z(e)$. The profit generated by the agent is $\pi(e, z)$ if the agent puts down the effort e and the random payoff is z. The agent has the cost $c(e)$ of putting down the effort e, and the payment to the agent is given by $s(z)$ if the random payoff is z. The agent's utility function is u_A, and the principal's utility function is u_P. With this set-up, we use the following expected utility functions for the agent and principal respectively:

- The agent's expected utility is the expected utility of the payment $s = s(Z(e))$, and then the cost $c = c(e)$ of the effort is subtracted from this:

$$E\left[u_A(s)\right] - c = E\left[u_A(s) - c\right].$$

- The principal's expected utility is the expected utility of the profit $\pi = \pi(e, Z(e))$ minus the payment s to the agent:

$$E\left[u_P(\pi - s)\right].$$

Note that the utility functions take monetary values as arguments, which is the reason why we subtract the agent's (non-monetary) cost after calculating the expected utility of the payoff s. The timing of the contractual situation between the principal and the agent is described in Figure 8.1.

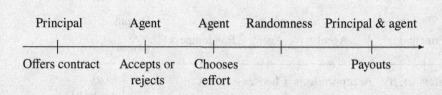

Figure 8.1: Timeline of a general contract situation.

8.3.1 Effort-dependent revenue

Consider a principal-agent situation where the agent puts down the effort e. This effort is obviously known by the agent, but we assume that it is not directly observable by the principal – only the output q generated by the agent is observed by the principal. We assume that

$$q = e + X,$$

where X is a random variable with $E(X) = 0$ and variance $\sigma^2(X) = \sigma_0^2$. We further assume that the cost for the agent of putting down the effort e is $c(e) = e^2/2$.

The wage $w(q)$ paid to the agent is set through a linear wage scheme,

$$w(q) = \alpha + \beta q = \alpha + \beta e + \beta X,$$

and the principal wants to choose α and β optimally (to be precisely defined below). The revenue for the principal is $p \cdot q$, and the cost is $w(q)$. We normalise the price of the output to $p = 1$. We further assume, as is common in these model, that the principal (e.g., a firm) is risk neutral, and that the agent is risk averse with constant coefficient of risk aversion equal to ρ.

Payoffs and attitudes towards risk		
	The principal	**The agent**
Payoff	$q - w(q)$	$w(q)$
Attitude towards risk	Risk neutral	Risk averse

In the language of the general model in Section 8.3 we have

$$
\begin{aligned}
Z &= e + X \\
s &= \alpha + \beta z \\
c &= \frac{e^2}{2} \\
\pi &= z.
\end{aligned}
$$

The timing is as follows: First the principal chooses α and β, and given these values the agent chooses the effort e. See Figure 8.2 for the timeline in this case. As in other sequential situations, e.g., in the Stackelberg oligopoly model, we start from the back, i.e. with the agent.

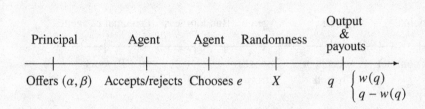

Figure 8.2: Timeline of a specific contract situation.

The goal for the agent is to choose e in order to maximise the expected utility

$$E\left[u_A(w(q))\right] - e^2/2.$$

We now use the approximate certainty equivalent formula (or, equivalently, assume that X is normally distributed) in order to calculate the certainty equivalent $CE(e)$ of $w(q)$.

$$
\begin{aligned}
CE(e) &= E(w(q)) - \frac{\rho}{2}\sigma^2(w(q)) \\
&= E(\alpha + \beta e + \beta X) - \frac{\rho}{2}\sigma^2(\alpha + \beta e + \beta X) \\
&= \alpha + \beta e - \frac{\rho}{2}\beta^2\sigma_0^2.
\end{aligned}
$$

To simplify, we assume that the agent wants to maximise[1]

$$CE(e) - \frac{e^2}{2}.$$

In order for the agent to find the optimal effort, the agent sets the derivative of this expression with respect to e equal to zero:

$$CE'(e) - e = 0 \iff \beta - e = 0 \implies e = \beta.$$

It follows that at the optimal point $e = \beta$, the utility for the agent is given by

$$CE(\beta) - \frac{\beta^2}{2} = \alpha + \beta \cdot \beta - \frac{\rho}{2}\beta^2\sigma_0^2 - \frac{\beta^2}{2} = \alpha + \frac{\beta^2}{2}(1 - \rho\sigma_0^2).$$

The principal wants to maximise the expected value (since he or she is risk neutral) of the output minus the wage:

$$E(q - w(q)) = E(e + X - (\alpha + \beta e + \beta X)) = e - (\alpha + \beta e).$$

---

[1]This can be justified using Taylor expansions. Alternatively, we can assume that the cost $e^2/2$ *is* measured in monetary units and write $E[u_A(w(q) - e^2/2)]$.

We know from above that whatever values of α and β, the agent will choose the effort level $e = \beta$; this is the *incentive compatibility constraint*. Hence, the expected profit is

$$\beta - (\alpha + \beta \cdot \beta) = \beta - \alpha - \beta^2. \tag{8.1}$$

The monetary value for the agent of not working is CE_0, and this leads to the *participation constraint*

$$\alpha + \frac{\beta^2}{2}(1 - \rho\sigma_0^2) \geq CE_0.$$

From now on we assume that $CE_0 = 0$. The maximising problem for the principal is thus

$$\max_{\alpha, \beta} \beta - \alpha - \beta^2 \text{ such that } \alpha + \frac{\beta^2}{2}(1 - \rho\sigma_0^2) \geq 0.$$

To continue, we observe that the principal wants to minimise its cost, hence choosing as low α and β that satisfies the participation constraint. Hence, at the optimal choice of (α, β), the inequality will be an equality (there is no need to pay the agent more than the certainty equivalent c_0):

$$\alpha + \frac{\beta^2}{2}(1 - \rho\sigma_0^2) = 0.$$

By solving for α we get

$$\alpha = \frac{\beta^2}{2}(\rho\sigma_0^2 - 1).$$

We now insert this in Equation (8.1) of the expected profit of the firm:

$$\beta - \alpha - \beta^2 = \beta + \frac{\beta^2}{2}(1 - \rho\sigma_0^2) - \beta^2 = \beta - \frac{\beta^2}{2}(1 + \rho\sigma_0^2).$$

This is the expression which the firm wants to maximise in order to find the β that is optimal for the principal. The first-order condition for the principal is

$$1 - \beta(1 + \rho\sigma_0^2) = 0 \implies \beta = \frac{1}{1 + \rho\sigma_0^2}.$$

Inserting this into the participation contraint yields

$$\alpha = -\frac{\left(\frac{1}{1+\rho\sigma_0^2}\right)^2}{2}(1 - \rho\sigma_0^2) = \frac{\rho\sigma_0^2 - 1}{2(1 + \rho\sigma_0^2)^2}.$$

With this choice of α and β, and with $e = \beta$, the expected profit (here, again, we use that the principal is risk neutral) of the principal is

$$E(q - w(q)) = \frac{1}{1 + \rho v} \cdot \left(1 - \frac{1}{1 + \rho\sigma_0^2}\right) - \left(-\frac{1 - \rho\sigma_0^2}{2(1 + \rho\sigma_0^2)^2}\right) = \frac{1}{2} \cdot \frac{1}{1 + \rho\sigma_0^2}.$$

In this case the expected profit is always positive. If, however, the certainty equivalent CE_0 is strictly positive and large, then the expected profit can be negative, and the principal will not offer any contract. We can now summarise the solution:

1) The principal (leader) sets

$$\alpha = \frac{\rho\sigma_0^2 - 1}{2(1 + \rho\sigma_0^2)^2} \quad \text{and} \quad \beta = \frac{1}{1 + \rho\sigma_0^2}.$$

2) The agent (follower) chooses the effort level

$$e = \frac{1}{1 + \rho\sigma_0^2}.$$

Before moving to the next model, we make the following observations.

- The principal sets the value of β in order to make the agent to put the effort equal to β, the incentive compatibility constraint, and chooses α in order to fulfil the participating constraint.

- The value of β satisfies $0 < \beta \leq 1$. The value of $\beta = 1$ is achieved when $\rho = 0$ or when $\sigma_0 = 0$, i.e. when either the agent is risk-neutral or when there is no randomness in the observed effort.

8.3.2 Effort-dependent cost

A contractor is being hired to complete a construction project whose value to the buyer of the contractor's services is equal to the value v (a known constant). The initial cost of the project is $C_0 + \varepsilon$, where ε is a random variable with $E(\varepsilon) = 0$ and $\sigma^2(\varepsilon) = \sigma_0^2 > 0$. By putting down the effort e, the cost of the project diminishes to

$$C(e) = C_0 - e,$$

and the cost of putting down effert e is $c(e) = e^2/2$. The realised cost of the project

$$C(e) + \varepsilon = C_0 - e + \varepsilon$$

is verifiable, and the payout s to the contractor is given by

$$s = \alpha + \beta(C(e) + \varepsilon) = \alpha + \beta(C_0 - e + \varepsilon).$$

In the language of the general model in Section 8.3 we have

$$\begin{aligned}
Z &= C_0 - e + \varepsilon \\
s &= \alpha + \beta z \\
c &= \frac{e^2}{2} \\
\pi &= v.
\end{aligned}$$

The contractor is assumed to be risk averse with constant coefficient of risk-aversion ρ, and the buyer is assumed to be risk neutral. The calculations in this model are similiar to the ones in the previous section, and they are put in Appendix A.9. Instead we only present the summary of the solution here.

1) The principal (leader) sets

$$\alpha = \frac{1}{1 + \rho\sigma_0^2} \left(C_0 + \frac{\rho\sigma_0^2 - 1}{2(\rho\sigma_0^2 + 1)} \right) \quad \text{and} \quad \beta = \frac{\rho\sigma_0^2}{1 + \rho\sigma_0^2}.$$

2) The agent (follower) chooses the effort level

$$e = \frac{1}{1 + \rho\sigma_0^2}.$$

This section is based on Olsen & Osmundsen [41], where, as the main model, they consider the model we have presented with *endogenous* risk added to it. We will now present the model with endogenous risk, and some of it's results, but refer the reader to the paper Olsen & Osmundsen [41] for proofs and a more thorough analysis.

In the original model, the level of risk, as measured by the standard deviation, is determined within the model, and not given as a constant σ_0. This is done in the following way: The contract between the contractor and the buyer of the services of the contractor, has a parameter τ reflecting the degree of *specification* of the contract. The higher the value of τ, the more is the contract specified, and the level of specificity is reflected in the size of the variance of ε:

$$E\left[\varepsilon\right] = 0 \quad \text{and} \quad \sigma^2(\varepsilon) = \frac{\sigma_0^2}{1 + \tau}.$$

On the other hand, we know that it is costly to write specific contracts. In this model, the cost of having the level of specificity τ is $d(\tau)$. With this specification, we get the following optimal behaviour:

1) The principal (buyer) sets

$$\alpha = \frac{1}{1 + \rho\sigma_0^2} \left(C_0 + \frac{\rho\sigma_0^2 - 1}{2(\rho\sigma_0^2 + 1)} \right) \quad \text{and} \quad \beta = \frac{\rho\sigma_0^2}{1 + \tau + \rho\sigma_0^2}.$$

2) The agent (contractor) chooses the effort level

$$e = \frac{1}{1 + \tau + \rho\sigma_0^2}.$$

Note that when $\tau = 0$, then we are back to the solution without endogenous risk, and as τ increases, both β and e tend to zero.

8.3.3 Unknown cost function

A municipality is contracting a developer to build a number of residental properties. The developer's cost function is given by

$$C = \beta - e,$$

where β is a parameter, and e is the effort. The lower the value of β, the lower is the cost of putting down effort e, and hence, the more efficient is the developer. The municipality cannot observe the effort e, but it can observe the cost C. The developer is paid the cost by the municipality, and the cost for the developer to use effort e is $g(e) = e^2/2$. The utility for a developer that accepts an offer from the municipality is

$$U = T - g(e) = T - g(\beta - C).$$

If the value of β is known, then the municipality would offer a contract of the form $(T(\beta), c(\beta))$, where the amount $T(\beta)$ is transferred to the developer, and $c(\beta)$ is the cost that the developer is allowed to use on the production of the building project. Since C is observed, the fact that β is known implies that also e is known (since $e = \beta - C$). Hence, it is more reasonable to assume the municipality does not know the exact value of β. Instead we assume that beta can take one of two values: β_H or β_L with $\beta_H < \beta_L$. It follows that a developer with β_H is more efficient than a developer with β_L. The fraction of highly efficient firms, i.e. firms with β_H, is α.

In order to distinguish the two firms, the municipality wants to offer two different contracts[2]:

$$(T_H, c_H) \text{ and } (T_L, c_L).$$

the municipality wants a firm with β_H to choose (T_H, c_H), and a firm with β_L to choose (T_L, c_L). In order for this to be true, we must impose the following two incentive compatibility constraints:

$$T_H - g\left(\boxed{\beta_H} - c_H\right) \geq T_L - g\left(\boxed{\beta_H} - c_L\right)$$

and

$$T_L - g\left(\boxed{\beta_L} - c_L\right) \geq T_H - g\left(\boxed{\beta_L} - c_H\right).$$

Here we have boxed β_H and β_L to emphasise that the first equation is the incentive compatibility constraint for a firm with β_H, and the second equation is the incentive compatibility constraint for a firm with β_L. We further assume that all developers' utility of not building the project is zero, so we get the following two participating constraints:

$$U_H = T_H - g(\beta_H - c_H) \geq 0$$

and

$$U_L = T_L - g(\beta_L - c_L) \geq 0.$$

To continue we make the following observation: The municipality would like to reward an efficient firm, i.e. a firm with β_H, if this type of firm is offered to realise the building project, but it would not like to reward an inefficient firm. For this reason it wants to choose contracts such that the utility of an inefficient firm is zero:

$$U_L = T_L - g(\beta_L - c_L) = 0,$$

and such that the incentive compatibility constraint is fulfilled for the efficient firm:

$$T_H - g(\beta_H - c_H) = T_L - g(\beta_H - c_L).$$

The value of the building project for the municipality is v, and the cost for the municipality is $c + T$. In order to raise the money to pay the developer, the municipality needs to borrow money at rate r, hence, the actual cost for the municipality is $-(1 + r) \cdot (c + T)$. The total value of the building project is

---

[2]Here and in the following we shorten the notation by letting $T_H = T(\beta_H)$, $c_H = c(\beta_H)$, $T_L = T(\beta_L)$ and $c_L = T(\beta_L)$.

[The net value for the municipality] + [The net value for the developer] =

$$[v - (1+r) \cdot (c(\beta) + T(\beta))] + [T(\beta) - g(\beta - c(\beta))] =$$
$$v - (1+r)c(\beta) - rT(\beta) - g(\beta - c(\beta)).$$

Since the fraction of efficient firms is α, the expected value of this (which is the value for a risk-neutral society) is

$$v - \alpha((1+r)c_H + rT_H + g(\beta_H - c_H)) - (1-\alpha)((1+r)c_L + rT_L + g(\beta_L - c_L)).$$

The two equality constraints argued for above, can be written

$$\begin{aligned} T_L &= g(\beta_L - c_L) \\ T_H &= g(\beta_H - c_H) + g(\beta_L - c_L) - g(\beta_H - c_L). \end{aligned}$$

Replacing T_L and T_H with these two expressions result in the following first-order conditions with respect to c_H and c_L respectively:

$$\begin{aligned} \beta_H - c_H &= 1 \\ \beta_L - c_L &= 1 - \frac{r}{1+r} \cdot \frac{\alpha}{1-\alpha} \cdot (\beta_L - \beta_H). \end{aligned}$$

See Appendix A.10 for a derivation of this. Since $e = \beta - C$, we can write these two equations as

$$\begin{aligned} e_H &= 1 \\ e_L &= 1 - \frac{r}{1+r} \cdot \frac{\alpha}{1-\alpha} \cdot (\beta_L - \beta_H). \end{aligned}$$

Furthermore,

$$\frac{r}{1+r} \cdot \frac{\alpha}{1-\alpha} \cdot (\beta_L - \beta_H) > 0$$

from which it follows that $e_L < e_H$.

Although this is a contractual situation, it is "technically one of adverse selection even though it apparently mixes adverse selection and moral hazard elements" (Laffont & Tirole [30] p. 106). The situation is depicted in Figure 8.3. The following parameter values were used in the figure:

$$\alpha = 0.25, \ r = 0.02, \ \beta_H = 1.25 \text{ and } \beta_L = 2.$$

These values result in the municipality offering the following two contracts:

$$(c_H, T_H) = (0.25, 0.936) \text{ and } (c_L, T_L) = (1.044, 0.457),$$

as can be seen in the figure. The efforts put down are

$$e_H = 1 \text{ and } e_L = 0.956$$

respectively. What's happening here is that the two contracts are constructed so that the inefficient firm prefers one contract to the other; in Figure 8.3 utility is increasing in the north-east direction. The efficient firm is indifferent between the two contracts, so we can posit that an efficient firm will choose the contract not chosen by the inefficient firm.

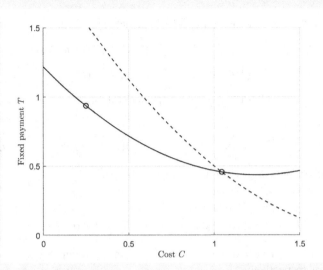

Figure 8.3: Contracts in situations with unknown cost.

8.4   First-best solutions

In this section we introduce the concept of a *first-best solution*. This is the solution you get if the agent and principal work together, and typically it is the result you get if you assume that effort is observable. Although often not a realistic outcome, it is the best possible outcome, and it could be interesting to compare the first-best solution with the solution you get when the effort is not observable. In the following sections we calculate the first-best solutions for the models from Sections 8.3.1, 8.3.2 and 8.3.3.

8.4.1   Effort-dependent revenue

Recalling the model from Section 8.3.1, if the effort e is observable, then the wage can get set according to

$$w(e) = \alpha + \beta e.$$

But we see that this is the same model as if we assume that $\sigma^2(\varepsilon) = 0$. Hence, we can use the same formulas as we derived in Section 8.3.1 and setting $\sigma^2(\varepsilon) = \sigma_0^2 = 0$ in them. This results in the following special case of the summary from Section 8.3.1:

1) The principal (leader) sets

$$\alpha = CE_0 - \frac{1}{2} \quad \text{and} \quad \beta = 1.$$

2) The agent (follower) chooses the effort level

$$e = 1.$$

8.4.2 Effort-dependent cost

When effort is observable, the payout can be written as a function of the effort e. Assuming a linear payout scheme, the payout to the contractor is

$$s = \alpha + \beta e.$$

As in the section above on effort-dependent revenue, we get the first-best solution by setting $\sigma^2(\varepsilon) = \sigma_0^2 = 0$. This results in the following first-best solution:

1) The principal (leader) sets

$$\alpha = C_0 - \frac{1}{2} \quad \text{and} \quad \beta = 0.$$

2) The agent (follower) chooses the effort level

$$e = 1.$$

8.4.3 Unknown cost function

When there is full information, this case is a Stackelberg situation where the society chooses a contract that is optimal from its perspective. The quantity the society wants to maximise is

$$v - (1 + r)c(\beta) - rT(\beta) - g(\beta - c(\beta)).$$

With known β we can replace $c(\beta)$ with $\beta - e$, resulting in

$$v - (1 + r)(\beta - e) - rT(\beta) - g(e).$$

Furthermore, the society wants the developer to participate, but not pay it more then necessary. Since the reservation utility of the developer is 0, this means that the society wants to impose

$$0 = U = T - g(e) \quad \Leftrightarrow \quad T = g(e).$$

This leads

$$v - (1 + r)(\beta - e + g(e))$$

to be maximised. Setting the derivative of this to zero results in

$$(1 + r)(1 - g'(e)) = 0 \quad \Leftrightarrow \quad g'(e) = 1.$$

Since $g(e) = e^2/2$, we have $g'(e) = e$, so the first-best solution is $e = 1$.

8.5   Methods to avoid moral hazard

In principal-agent relationships, the risks emerging from information asymmetry and conflicting interests after signing a contract can be reduced in several ways. Most commonly, that includes bureaucratic control through contracts, incentives (bonuses), information systems for monitoring performance, as well as "soft" factors like corporate culture, trust and reputation (Ceric [7]).

8.5.1 Contract structures and incentives

One of the primary tools to reduce moral hazard in a principal-agent relationship is the harmonisation of economic interests. Depending on the contract type, there are several ways in which the surplus (profit) of the collaboration can be divided (recall the Box on page 98). Construction projects can be delivered in a variety of contract formats with different risk/profit allocation mechanisms.

- *Design-bid-build* ("DBB", designer and contractor hired separately by project owner).

- *Design-build* ("DB", designer and contractor hired by owner as single entity under one contract).

- *Construction manager at risk* ("CMR", project manager hired by owner as consultant to coordinate and oversee the delivery of the project).

- *Integrated project delivery* ("IPD", single contract for design and construction with a shared risk/reward model).

If also the operation or financing of a project are included in the tendering scope, additional set-ups can be considered, but will not be examined further here. Instead, we will focus on a DB structure as the most common approach.

Let us look at the different payment methods applicable in a DB setting. If the client as principal and the contractor as agent agree on a *fixed-fee contract* (lump-sum price), the cost (and schedule) risk is mostly with the contractor without any incentive to optimise the project efficiency. If its own costs (e.g., materials, subcontractors, etc.) are higher than initially expected, the contractor will try to compromise on quality or claim additional costs. On the other hand, if the costs are lower than expected, there is no incentive to work efficiently because the remuneration will be the same. In the case of a *piecewise contract* using unit or hourly rates, the contractor will not compromise on quality and is less vulnerable to price increases and change orders by the project owner. Instead, the client has a much larger risk of incurring higher costs unless there is a clearly defined threshold (guaranteed maximum cost). In both cases, the interests of the client and the contractor are not aligned and it may be that the lack of transparency encourages opportunistic behaviour of either of the parties. A way to harmonise the respective interests and share the project risks is the introduction of a target cost approach or *sharing contract*. Estimating the exact target costs up front and linking the contractor payment to the overall project costs provides significant cost control and innovation incentives and makes it no longer attractive for individual project members to pursue only their own interests (Schieg [46]). The target cost is the cost to the contractor of completing the project, i.e., the base cost of the physical works (based on the sum of prices in a bill of quantities, schedule of rates or an activity schedule, and including cost of temporary works, subcontractor costs and preliminary costs), overheads and profit, and a contingency for the contractor's risks under the contract. Upon completion of the project, a mechanism is used to calculate whether savings were made (project costs < target cost), or whether costs overran (project costs > target cost). The contractor will then either share the savings with the principal or contribute towards the overspend.

In the context of construction projects – which are temporary in nature – it is also worth looking beyond a single project to a more long-term partnering set-up. This allows for an early contractor involvement and the opportunity to adjust contractual agreements over time as part of a continuous learning and improvement process (Eriksson, Atkin & Nilsson [14]).

8.5.2   Information systems and performance monitoring

In the operation phase of a building, the facility manager has to maintain and repair the building equipment in an efficient and effective manner. To do so, he or she has to make estimates about the likeliness and the impact of a system failure. Maintenance intervals are determined to monitor the status of the building equipment and thus prevent breakdowns. This allows the manager to not check the equipment every day and can dedicate his or her time to other activities. It may however still be the case that even if the facility manager performs frequent checks, a system will eventually or due to an external shock stop working. Likewise, even if the manager performs poorly and skips a few maintenance intervals to save time, staff and therefore costs, the building equipment does not immediately fail. Hence, based only on the observation of a system as working or not, it is difficult to remunerate the facility manager for the performance of services (as the "input" does not directly equal the "output", but includes a random variable). Again, this is taken into consideration for the set-up of the principal-agent relationship and the avoidance of moral hazards. On the one hand, this concerns the contract mechanisms and incentive structures as discussed in the previous chapter. On the other hand, formal planning and control systems to track and assess performance create more transparency with regard to the actions of the project participants. In this regard, relevant tools for the principal, this is based on Atkin & Brooks [2] pp. 192 ff. and Páez-Pérez & Sánchez-Silva [42], include the following.

- Monitoring and reporting:

  - End-user satisfaction (e.g., based on occupancy surveys).

  - Regulatory compliance.

  - Quality- and performance-related targets.

  - Expenditure-related targets.

  - Time-related targets.

- Benchmarking:

  - Against other market actors.

  - Against comparable buildings.

- Audits and reviews:

  - Regular client inspections

  - Performance review meetings

  - Ad-hoc checks by principal or external auditor

An increasing role is being played by technology in this context, for instance through CAFM (computer-aided facility management) systems, digital building models and sensors, or a combination of those solutions (Atkin & Brooks [2], pp. 302 ff.). Leveraging real-time building data and documentation reduces the reliance on human estimations and implicit knowledge of individual workers. It also helps to make information more transparent to all stakeholders and in consequence to avoid opportunistic behaviour.

8.5.3 Trust and relationship building

Last but not least, the frequency of the cooperation of the project participants is of major importance. If the contractual partners repeatedly cooperate with one another, the resulting mutual trust can lead to a reduction of information asymmetry and opportunistic behaviour. The example of property valuation is used to briefly illustrate the impact of relationship-building on risk mitigation and optimised performance.

Property appraisals are performed in a number of cases, both as a one-off task during an asset transaction, and on a regular (annual, quarterly, ...) basis as part of the risk management in commercial real estate investment. The valuer hired uses market and property information to determine the market value of an asset. Here, several biases can occur that lead to a suboptimal result from a general welfare perspective. For instance, upwardly biased appraised values of residential properties contributed to the 2008 financial crisis (Eriksen et al. [13]). Examples of asymmetric information and opportunistic behaviour of either the principal or the agent include but are not limited to:

- Confirmation bias: If the previous valuation result or contract value is known to the valuer, he or she is likely to search for information confirming that pre-defined assumption as a result of cognitive bias. Deviating information may be ignored or underweighted.

- Conditional fees: If a valuer's compensation is conditional to successful loan originations (e.g., in housing transactions prior to the financial crisis in 2008) or transaction completions or represents a share of the property's market value, there is another incentive to provide confirmatory valuations and thus avoid fee reductions.

- Client influence: Clients with expertise and a high level of knowledge of the property market are able to influence valuers through expert, information and procedural power (Kamalahasan [27]). For instance, fund managers have incentives to influence valuations, as these are used as performance metrics (Baum et al. [3]). Opportunities to exert influence are afforded by the control a (larger) client has over the valuation process, including the common practice of reviewing draft valuations prior to their formalisation (Levy & Schuck [32])

If performed as a one-off task (static game, as introduced in Chapter 2), both parties in an appraisal process will likely act in their own best interest and might show opportunistic behaviour. However, in a long-term relationship (/dynamic game), non-cooperative behaviour can be punished by the other party, making mutual trust and a good reputation far more important than short-term wins.

Codes of conduct and industry guidelines such as the RICS Red Book highlight potential conflicts of interest to be avoided, such as "acting for the buyer and the seller of a property or asset in the same transaction, acting for two or more parties competing for an opportunity, [. . .] and undertaking a valuation for third-party consumption where the valuer's firm has other fee-earning relationships with the client".[3] Moreover, it is considered good practice to rotate valuers after a maximum of seven years in an attempt to counteract client pressure and ensure market-conform valuations.[4] Last but not least, automated property valuations and the use of artificial intelligence in market analyses aim to further eliminate opportunistic behaviour of human market actors.

---

[3]https://www.rics.org/globalassets/rics-website/media/upholding-professional-standards/sector-standards/valuation/rics-valuation–global-standards-jan.pdf p. 21.

[4]https://www.rics.org/globalassets/rics-website/media/upholding-professional-standards/sector-standards/valuation/rics-valuation–global-standards-jan.pdf p. 25.

8.6 Literature notes

For a general introduction to hidden actions and moral hazard, see Perloff [43], Varian [53] or Hendrikse [22]. The general model in Section 8.3 is taken from Hart & Holmström [21], which contains a good introduction to general contract theory. The model in Section 8.3.2 is based on Olsen & Osmundsen [41].

8.7 Exercises

Exercise 8.1 For the development of a new urban area, the city council appoints a consulting company to support the design of a planning strategy. The consulting company's profit as a function of the observable effort (e.g., billable hours of work, delivery of project milestones) is

$$\pi(e) = 5e - e^2 - w(e).$$

The salary paid to the consultancy's project manager is $w(e) = e$, and the cost for the project manager when the effort e is put down is $c(e) = e^2/2$.

a) What is the optimal level of effort from the company's point of view?

b) What is the optimal level of effort from the project manager's point of view?

In order to align the incentives of the project manager with the company, the company wants to change from the present salary to the linear salary scheme

$$w(e) = \alpha + \beta e.$$

c) Show that in this case the optimal level for the project manager is $e = \beta$.

d) Show that in order for the project manager to accept the new salary scheme it must satisfy

$$\alpha + \frac{\beta^2}{2} \geq \frac{1}{2}.$$

This will be the participation constraint.

e) Use the results from c) and d) above to write the company's profit as a function of β, i.e. write $\pi = \pi(\beta)$, and find the optimal value of β for the firm.

f) How should the company choose α?

Exercise 8.2 An employee that puts down the effort e is producing the output $q = 3e + X$, where X is a random variable with mean 0 and variance 4. The salary of the employee is given by

$$w(q) = 1 + 2q,$$

and the cost for the employee to put down the effort e is

$$c(e) = 3e^2.$$

The certainty equivalent for the employee of not working is $CE_0 = 0$. The random payoff Y if the employee puts down the effort e and the quantity q is produced is

$$Y = w(q) - c(e) = 1 + 2q - 3e^2.$$

Determine the optimal level of effort, and if the employee will put down this effort, in the following cases:

a) The employee values a random payoff Y according to the formula

$$E(Y) - \sigma^2(Y).$$

b) The employee is risk-neutral.

Chapter 9

Property rights

In this concluding chapter, we show how contracts and clear definitions of power and control further support efficient interactions of different industry stakeholders in the best societal interest. The concept of externalities, property rights and vertical integration are introduced, building upon among other things the theoretical foundations of welfare from Chapter 1.

9.1 Externalities

An *externality* is consequence of an action that influences the decisions of an individual or a firm indirectly, and not directly through a market and changes in prices. This means that in general, the market cannot solve the efficient allocation of the externality.

Externalities

- A *positive externality* is beneficial for others. An example is art or a park in connection to an office building.

- A *negative externality* harms others. The typical example of a negative externality is pollution.

We remark that an externality can in fact be positive to some, and negative to others. Although positive externalities exist, we will focus on negative externalities. From an economic point of view, the problem with negative externalities is that they are produced in a quantity that is too large from a welfare perspective. The reason for this is that the firms' *private cost* is lower than the *social cost*. The reverse holds for a positive externality: Too little is produced and the private cost is higher than the social cost.

On a competitive market, firms pollute the environment through carbon emissions when they produce their good. The firms' aggregated *private* marginal cost function is given by

$$MC^P(Q) = 3Q,$$

and the inverse demand function by

$$p(Q) = 100 - Q.$$

The competitive equilibrium quantity Q_c satisfies

$$MC^P(Q_c) = p(Q_c) \quad \Leftrightarrow \quad 3Q_c = 100 - Q_c \quad \Rightarrow \quad Q_c = \frac{100}{4} = 25.$$

The pollution creates a marginal cost for the society of Q, so the *social* marginal cost is equal to

$$MC^s(Q) = MC^P + Q = 3Q + Q = 4Q.$$

The society wants to take all the costs into account, so the society want the quantity Q_s satisfying

$$MC^s(Q_s) = p(Q_s)$$

to be produced. This quantity satisfies

$$4Q_s = 100 - Q_s \quad \Rightarrow \quad Q_s = \frac{100}{5} = 20,$$

and we note that

$$20 = Q_s \leq Q_c = 25.$$

The situation so far is depicted in Figure 9.1.

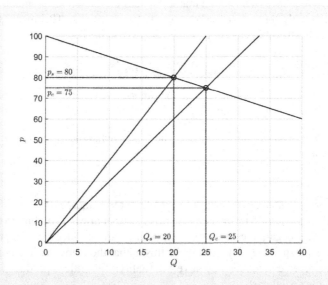

Figure 9.1: Equilibria with a negative externality.

Since the society takes the firms' cost as well as the cost for the pollution into account, the socially optimal outcome is $Q_s = 20$. Hence, if a quantity other than this is produced, there will be a deadweight loss. In this case, the deadweight loss DWL is the triangle with corners at the stars in Figure 9.2

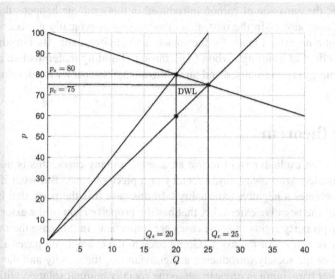

Figure 9.2: Deadweight loss.

If the property rights are not well defined, there is a way for the society to achieve the socially optimal level, and that is by introducing a tax. In this pollution example, the tax per unit produced should be 20. With this tax, the producers profit maximisation condition is

$$3Q_{\text{tax}} + 20 = 100 - Q_{\text{tax}} \implies Q_{\text{tax}} = 20.$$

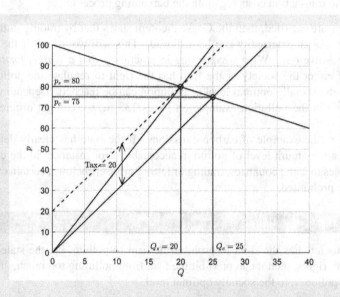

Figure 9.3: Equilibria with taxes.

See Figure 9.3 for a graphical depiction of this. This kind of tax is known as a *Pigouvian tax*. In real estate, the emission of carbon introduced in this example happens through building construction and operations. In the past, this externality was typically not accounted for even though it comes at a negative impact for the society and environment. By introducing a carbon tax, the negative effect of emitting carbon (e.g. through building materials like concrete or the consumption of energy) is internalised and turns into a tangible cost for the developer or building owner.

9.2   Coase theorem

A *property right* is an exclusive right to use an asset. In many cases, this is not a problem in the sense that it is clear who owns, say, a factory or a piece of land. But what if the factory or the piece of land creates a negative externality? In this case it is the party that has the right to control the level of the negative externality that has the property right of the externality, and this is the reason why property rights in some cases are important. In this case the ownership of an asset gives *power* or *control* of the asset. Going back to the example on pages 133 ff. of a firm polluting, instead of the society introducing a Pigouvian tax, the society and the firms can start to bargain. Whether bargaining in order to get to the socially optimal solution will work or not is depending on well-defined property rights and how costly the bargaining is.

An important result regarding the possibility of reaching the socially optimal solution by using bargaining is the *Coase theorem*, which was first presented in Coase [9]. This result holds under the following (strong) conditions.

- It is possible to bargain.

- Property rights are well defined.

- There are no transaction costs regading the bargaining process.

If these conditions are satisifed, then the Coase theorem states that by trading in the externality, the optimal level of a an externality can be achieved. This will work both if the externality is a negative or a positive one. What's happening in practice is that *a market for the externality is introduced*. If either the society or the firm has the right to regulate the pollution, then an agreement about the socially optimal level of pollution can be reached. Depending on who has the property rights in the pollution example on pages 133 ff., we can get different bargaining outcomes.

Let us return to the example of carbon emissions. If the state has clearly defined property rights, it can set a maximum level of pollution acceptable. For instance, in the case of energy consumption passes in some countries, trading or letting of assets below a certain efficiency level is or will soon be prohibited.

The property rights of polluting

- If *the society* has the right to prohibit the firm to pollute, i.e. the state owns the property rights, then it can prohibit the firm from polluting too much, and thereby set the pollution to the socially optimal level.

- If *the firm* has the right to pullute, i.e. the firm owns the property rights, then it can accept money from the society in order to decrease pollution to the socially optimal level.

We end this section on the Coase theorem by a quotation from the original paper Coase [9]. In the quote, who is "liable or not for a damage caused" is decided through well-defined property rights.

> "It is necessary to know whether the damaging business is liable or not for damage caused since without the establishment of this initial delimitation of rights there can be no market transactions to transfer and recombine them. But the ultimate result (which maximises the value of production) is independent of the legal position if the pricing system is assumed to work without cost." (Coase [9], p. 8.)

9.3 Hold-up problem

If two parties decide to jointly realise a project (with one party hiring/contracting the other), they typically enter into a contractual agreement prior to the production of the good or provision of the service. From that moment onwards, their respective project success is depending on their willingness to cooperate. However, since it will be impossible to define all project parameters in the contract, there is a risk of the hiring party aiming to renegotiate the contract. In that case it might happen that the initial costs for the hired party are no longer sufficiently covered and it might be forced to accept the lower remuneration. This unbalanced allocation of bargaining power is called the *hold-up problem*. It is problematic, because in anticipation of its opponent's future step and without the respective contractual mechanisms, the hired party may underinvest, leading to an inefficient performance from the society's perspective.

To understand the implications in more detail, consider the following example. A property developer wants to build a residential building at a specific site. Upon completion, the building is expected to be acquired by an investor for €150m (= project value to the developer). To realise this project, a general contractor is chosen to design and build the property as a turnkey project at a cost of €100m (= project value to the contractor). To do so, the general contractor has to work with subcontractors on its own risk and costs. These costs are referred to as sunk costs, and their total value is denoted by k.

In the case of a successful project completion, the *surplus* is given by

$$\text{Surplus} = 150 - 100 = 50.$$

If the two companies have the same bargaining strength, the surplus could be split equally: the developer gets €25m and the general contractor gets €25m. Now assume that upon completion of the construction works, the developer refuses to pay the construction company and wants to renegotiate the agreement. If there is no agreement between both parties, the project value for the construction company at this point is $100 - k$. This means that the surplus that is to be divided has decreased. This new surplus is referred to as a *quasi-surplus*:

$$\text{Quasi-surplus} = 150 - (100 - k) = 50 + k.$$

If the developer succeeds in renegotiating the contract, then he or she will take into account that the construction company has had a sunk cost of k. Given equal bargain power, the developer can argue that the quasi-surplus should be shared 50/50, i.e. the division should be:

$$\text{Constructor's payoff} \quad = \quad -k + \frac{50 + k}{2} = 25 - \frac{k}{2}$$

$$\text{Developer's payoff} \quad = \quad \frac{50 + k}{2} = 25 + \frac{k}{2}$$

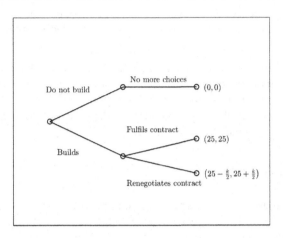

Figure 9.4: General hold-up problem.

Note that the total payoff is equal to the surplus. The purpose of the quasi-surplus is to define the *division* of the surplus. Given the fact that the developer can threaten to start bargaining after the investment of the sunk cost is done, means that before entering a contract with the developer, the contractor considers the game tree in Figure 9.4. If the sunk cost $k > 50$, then the construction company's payoff is negative:

$$\text{Contractor's payoff} = 25 - \frac{k}{2} < 0 \text{ when } k > 50.$$

In Figures 9.5 and 9.6 we give two examples of outcomes of the hold-up problem, the outcome depending on the value of k. In Figure 9.5, the sunk cost is $k = 30$. In this case, the subgame perfect is for the contractor to build and then for the developer to renegotiate the contract. The payoffs in this case are

$$\begin{aligned}
\text{Constructor's payoff} &= 25 - \frac{30}{2} = 10 \\
\text{Developer's payoff} &= 25 + \frac{30}{2} = 40.
\end{aligned}$$

In this case the project is carried out, even though the payoff to the contractor is lower (10) than the payoff in the case of an equal division of the surplus (25).

Now consider the case when the sunk cost $k = 60$. The situation is depicted in Figure 9.6. Now the subgame perfect equilibrium is for the contractor not to accept to build, and

$$\begin{aligned}
\text{Constructor's payoff} &= 0 \\
\text{Developer's payoff} &= 0.
\end{aligned}$$

Note that the residential building will not be built, even though the total surplus still is $50 > 0$. Even though this is the best possible individual outcome in this scenario, the overall payoff in the

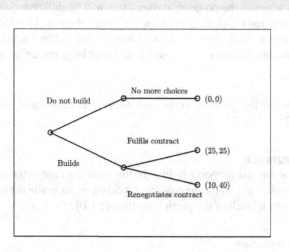

Figure 9.5: Hold-up problem I.

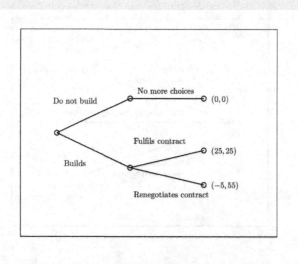

Figure 9.6: Hold-up problem II.

case of a project cancellation is not optimal, and the hold-up problem results in an outcome that is suboptimal from the society's perspective.

When can the developer force a renegotiation? The short answer is that the developer can renegotiate the contract when *property rights are not well defined*. If we introduce property rights, then, depending on who has the property rights, there will be different outcomes of the hold-up game. This is also referred to which *governance structure* there is. Hendrikse [22] defines three different governance structures: market, forward integration and backward integration. Here are the different governance structures in our model, and how large the different payoffs are.

- **Market**
  No specific player has property rights and the players have equal bargaining powers. The payoffs are $(25 - k/2, 25 + k/2)$.

- **Forward integration**
  The contractor has the property rights. In this case the contractor will take all the quasi-surplus $(= 50 + k)$ and receive the payoff $-k + 50 + k = 50$, while the payoff to the developer is 0. The payoffs to each of the parties are thus $(50, 0)$.

- **Backward integration**
  The developer has the property rights. In this case the developer takes the whole quasi-surplus of $k + 50$, i.e. the contractor is forced to take the full sunk cost. The payoffs in this case are $(-k, 50 + k)$.

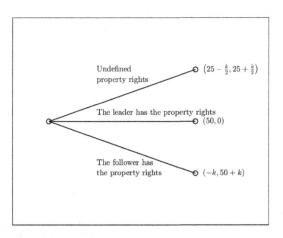

Figure 9.7: Governance structures with property rights.

These different choices are shown in Figure 9.7. From the society's perspective, it is not important how the surplus is divided. What *is* important is that if there is a positive surplus, then the investment yielding this positive surplus should be done. In the table below we have collected the cases where the socially optimal outcome is realised. It will depend both on the value of the sunk cost and on who, if any, has the property rights.

Hold-up problem with different sunk costs

This table shows when the socially optimal outcome can be achieved (Yes), and when in cannot (No).

Sunk cost	No property rights and equal bargaining power	The contractor has the property rights	The developer has the property rights
$k = 0$	Yes	Yes	Yes
$0 < k \leq 25$	Yes	Yes	No
$k > 25$	No	Yes	No

When $k = 0$, then the socially optimal outcome will always be the result independent of which governance structure prevails. This would be the outcome in a situation where the Coase theorem is valid. Also note that the contractor having the property rights is the preferred allocation from the society's point of view, since this will always lead to a socially optimal outcome. Finally we remark a way of solving the hold-up problem is if the two firms *integrate*, by which we mean that they form one firm. Again, as in the case of introducing a tax when there is a negative externality, the optimal choice is internalised within the firm. See Section 9.4 for more on this type of models.

What about sunk costs on the developer side? There are also costs that the developer incurs prior to project completion, such as overhead costs, land acquisition or financing costs, and those would be at risk as well if the project does not get realised. Consider extending the previous model, with a sunk cost k_0 for the developer. In this case

$$\text{Quasi-surplus} = (150 - k_0) - (100 - k) = 50 + k_0 + k,$$

and, assuming the "market" governance structure and thus a split of 50/50 of the quasi-surplus, the payoffs if the project is carried through are

$$\text{Constructor's payoff} = -k + \frac{50 + k_0 + k}{2} = 25 - \frac{k - k_0}{2}$$

$$\text{Developer's payoff} = -k_0 + \frac{50 + k_0 + k}{2} = 25 - \frac{k_0 - k}{2}.$$

Again, the surplus is 50, and the purpose of the quasi-surplus is to define the division of the surplus.

In Grossman & Hart [18], the distinction between *specific rights* and *residual rights* is made. Writing contracts is considered costly, and the difference between the two types of rights is that, although costly, specific rights are possible to be well defined in a contract. It is these costs that are the reason why contracts are interchanged with integration:

> "When it is too costly for one party to specify a long list of the particular rights it desires over another party's assets, it may be optimal for that party to purchase all the rights except those specifically mentioned in the contract." (Grossman & Hart [18], p. 692.)

If, as opposed to what is assumed in the Coase theorem, there are costs in connection with writing contracts, then we need to look at other solutions to the hold-up problem. One way is for the two firms entering into a contractual relationship to merge, and this is the topic of the next section.

9.4 Vertical integration

We have already briefly mentioned *vertical integration* in the Introduction to Chapter 6. Vertical integration is one type of *governance structure*. When contracts are complete, there is no need to specify the governance structure. An incomplete contract, on the other hand, means that there in general will be ex post bargaining. In this case, the choice of governance structure is important. One important question is what, when two firms choose to cooperate, this cooperation will look like. One firm can buy the other firm, they can create a joint venture, or the two firms can merge.

Consider a producer manufacturing a good that it sells to a retailer, who then, in turn sell this good to the consumers. The situation is depicted in Figure 9.8, which is a *vertically disintegrated* model. The producer is known as the *upstream firm*, and the retailer as the *downstream firm*. In this case, the retailer sets the price to the consumer, and the producer sets the price to the retailer. Since the retailer is a monopolist, this means that the retailer sets the quantity according

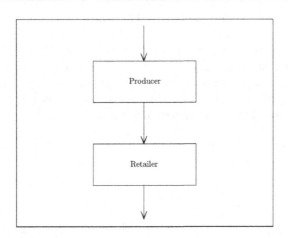

Figure 9.8: Upstream and downstream firm.

to $MR = MC$. This leads to a price to the consumers, which will depend on their demand function. To continue, the producer knows the demand for the good by the consumers, and also knows the price that the retailer will charge the consumers. This will in turn lead to the producer choosing the price to the retailer in order to maximise its profit. We assume a constant marginal cost for both the upstream and downstream firm, with c being the marginal cost for the producer, and that the fixed cost for both firms is zero. Futhermore, the consumers' demand function for the product sold by the retailer is

$$Q = 1 - p.$$

Given these assumptions, and with $0 < c < 1$ denoting the producer's marginal cost, we derive the following expressions in Appendix A.11.

Price and profits for two firms			
Consumers' price	Upstream firm's profit	Downstream firm's profit	Total profit
$\frac{3+c}{4}$	$\frac{(1-c)^2}{8}$	$\frac{(1-c)^2}{16}$	$\frac{3(1-c)^2}{16}$

If the two firms merge, then the firms are *vertically integrated*. One example of this set-up is when a real estate developer is building a residential property. In this case, the developer is the upstream firm and the company holding and managing the property is the downstream firm. The developer's business structure could aim to sell the completed property for the holding period ("trader developer") in which case the situation will be as in Figure 9.8 or it could set up an internal business unit to hold and manage the buildings ("investor developer"). In this case, there would be vertical integration as shown in Figure 9.9. What will happen with the price to the consumers

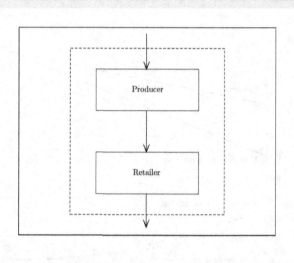

Figure 9.9: Collaboration in vertical integration.

and the profit if the firms choose to vertically integrate? This means that they work as one firm, with the cost of producing Q units equal to $c \cdot Q$, and the revenue equal to $p \cdot Q$. The vertically integrated firm is still a monopoly, now only *one* monopoly, so we get the optimal quantity for the vertically integrated firm by solving $MR = MC$. Since the inverse demand function is linear, we get

$$MR = 1 - 2Q$$

(see Section 1.4.2), and also

$$MC = c.$$

Hence,

$$MR = MC \quad \Leftrightarrow \quad 1 - 2Q = c \quad \Rightarrow \quad Q = \frac{1-c}{2}.$$

The price becomes

$$p = 1 - Q = 1 - \frac{1-c}{2} = \frac{1+c}{2},$$

and the profit of the vertically integrated firm is

$$\pi = p \cdot Q - c \cdot Q = \frac{1+c}{2} \cdot \frac{1-c}{2} - c \cdot \frac{1-c}{2} = \frac{(1-c)^2}{4}.$$

The results for the vertically integrated firm can be summarised as follows:

Price and profit for a vertically integrated firm

	Consumers' price	Profit
	$\frac{1+c}{2}$	$\frac{(1-c)^2}{4}$

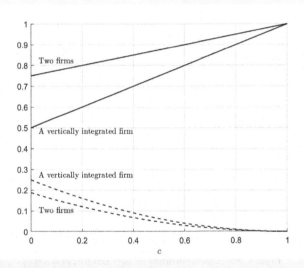

Figure 9.10: Market outcome of vertical integration.

In Figure 9.10 we show the difference in price (solid curves) and total profit (dashed curves) for the two cases. Note that the vertically integrated monopoly will make a larger profit than the total profit of the producer and the retailer when they are working as different companies, *and* the price the vertically integrated firm charges the consumer is lower than the price charged by the retailer without vertical integration. The fact that the two firms make a smaller total profit than the vertically integrated firm is due to fact that not forming a vertically integrated firm constitutes a negative externality. By creating a vertically integrating firm, this negative externality is no longer present and the reason for this is the same as in the case of introducing a tax when there is a negative externality: The externality is internalised.

It is interesting to compare this with the case when there is cooperation in an oligopoly. In that case (see Section 3.2.3), the total profit of the two firms increases, but the price to the consumers increases. The fact that this is not happening to the price set by the vertically integrated monopoly is again due to the fact that there is an elimination of a negative externality.

Despite the seemingly favourable outcome of vertical integration of firms, additional factors have to be taken into account when choosing the optimal set-up for a specific project. While reasonable from a purely economic perspective, vertical integration is not always the ideal solution from a management perspective. Different company cultures have to be merged carefully, processes will have to be aligned and some functions may become redundant as the result of the integration. It thus requires a holistic view to choosing the optimal governance structure beyond the underlying economic models and considerations. This could for example include long-term contracts, joint ventures, strategic alliances, technology licences, asset ownership and franchising. Those structures tend to involve lower capital costs and greater flexibility than vertical integration.

9.5 Literature notes

A general discussion externalities can be found in text books such as Perloff [43] or Varian [53]. For the hold-up problem and its connection to different government structures, see Hendrikse [22]. We also refer the reader to the academic papers mentioned in this chapter for more extensive descriptions.

9.6 Exercises

Exercise 9.1 How many subgames are there in the hold-up problem described in Figure 9.4? Motivate your answer.

Exercise 9.2 Show that the subgame perfect Nash equilibrium of the hold-up game in Figure 9.4 has the payoffs $(0, 0)$ when $k = 60$. What are the payoffs in the subgame perfect Nash equilibrium if $k = 20$?

Exercise 9.3 Consider the extended model in Section 9.3, where the developer also has a fixed cost k_0. Assume that this cost is $k_0 = 10$, and that the governance form is "market". For which values of the contractor's fixed cost k is the outcome that the project is realised?

Appendix A

Additional material

A.1 Derivatives

Let $f(x)$ be a function taking a number x and transforming it into the number $f(x)$. As a concrete example take the function $f(x) = 1 + 4x - x^2$. This function is plotted in Figure A.1.

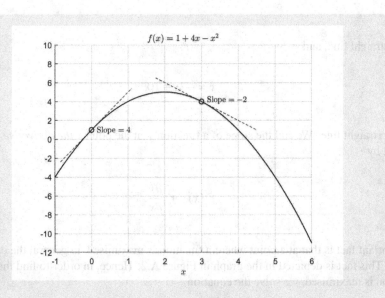

Figure A.1: Derivatives I.

We now ask the following question: What is the *slope* of the function at a point $(x, f(x))$? The slope of a function at the point $(x, f(x))$ is defined to be the slope of the straight line that is *tangental* to the function at the point $(x, f(x))$. For the function $f(x) = 1 + 4x - x^2$, the tangental lines of the function at the points $(0, 1)$ and $(3, 4)$ are plotted in the graph in Figure A.1. The equations for these two straight lines are

$$y = 4 + 1x,$$

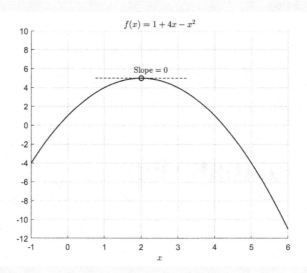

Figure A.2: Derivatives II.

the left straight line, and

$$y = -2x + 10,$$

the right straight line. We call the slope of a function f at the point x *the derivative of f at x*, and denote it by

$$f'(x) \quad \text{or} \quad \frac{df}{dx}.$$

An important fact is that at a point where a function is maximised, in general the derivative will be zero. This fact is depicted in the graph in Figure A.2. Hence, in order to find the point where a function is maximised, we solve the equation

$$f'(x) = 0.$$

Now, given that the derivative is an important tool in finding where a function, such as a utility function or a profit function, attains its maximum, it is important to be able to calculate the derivative. Here is a list of common derivatives that will be used in this book. The proof of these results lies outside the scope of this book, and we refer the reader to a book on basic calculus.

Common derivatives

$f(x)$	$f'(x)$ or $\frac{df}{dx}$
1	0
x	1
x^2	$2x$
x^3	$3x^2$
$\sqrt{x}$	$\frac{1}{2\sqrt{x}}$
$\frac{1}{\sqrt{x}}$	$-\frac{1}{2x^{3/2}}$
e^x	e^x
$\ln x$	$\frac{1}{x}$
$\frac{1}{x}$	$-\frac{1}{x^2}$

The following three rules are very useful when calculating derivatives.

Rules of the derivative

Rule 1

$$\left(f(x) + g(x)\right)' = f'(x) + g'(x),$$

or

$$\frac{d}{dx}(f+g) = \frac{df}{dx} + \frac{df}{dx}.$$

Rule 2

$$\left(f(x)g(x)\right)' = f'(x)g(x) + f(x)g'(x),$$

or

$$\frac{d}{dx}(fg) = \frac{df}{dx}g(x) + f(x)\frac{dg}{dx}.$$

Rule 3

$$\left(f(g(x))\right)' = f'(g(x)) \cdot g'(x),$$

or

$$\frac{d}{dx}(f(g(x))) = \frac{df}{dx}(g(x)) \cdot \frac{dg}{dx}(x)$$

Example A.1.1 Going back to the function $f(x) = 1 + 4x - x^2$ introduced at the beginning of this section, we see that

$$f'(x) = 0 + 4 - 2x = 4 - 2x.$$

Here, the 0 represents the fact that the derivative of a constant (in this case 1) is always equal to zero.

Finally we mention the notation of a *partial derivative*. If a function f has two variables, x_1 and

x_2, as inputs, then we can take the derivative both with respect to x_1 as well as with respect to x_2. We denote them

$$\frac{\partial f}{\partial x_1} \quad \text{and} \quad \frac{\partial f}{\partial x_2}$$

respectively. When calculating the partial derivative with respect to one variable, we consider all other variables as constants.

Example A.1.2 If

$$f(x_1, x_2) = x_1 x_2^2,$$

then

$$\frac{\partial f}{\partial x_1} = x_2^2$$

and

$$\frac{\partial f}{\partial x_2} = 2x_1 x_2.$$

A.2 Mixed strategies

In the main text we have only allowed for what are known as *pure strategies*. These are strategies that are known to the player using them before they are used. If the player instead chooses to randomise among a set of strategies, then this is known as a *mixed strategy*. Why would we be interested in this type of strategies? One answer is the following statement.

> **Nash equilibria in mixed strategies**
>
> If we allow for mixed strategies, then there always exists at least one Nash equilibrium in every static game with a finite number of players each having a finite number of actions to choose from.

An example of a game with no pure strategy Nash equilibrium is shown in Figure A.3.

		Player A	
		Strategy I	Strategy II
Player B	Strategy I	$(2, -2)$	$(-2, 2)$
	Strategy II	$(-2, 2)$	$(2, -2)$

Figure A.3: Pure strategies without Nash equilibria.

In this case the best response for each of the players is as follows.

For Player A:

- Player B chooses Strategy I → Player A chooses Strategy I.
- Player B chooses Strategy II → Player A chooses Strategy II.

For Player B:

- If Player A chooses Strategy I → Player B chooses Strategy II.
- If Player A chooses Strategy II → Player B chooses Strategy I.

By starting with Player B choosing Strategy I and following the chosen strategy by the other player, we see that there is no choice of strategies that a player does not want to deviate from. Hence, there exists no Nash equilibrium (in pure strategies).

A.3   Behavioural game theory

The basic models in game theory assume that all players behave in a rational way. Empirical studies, however, show that in experiments individuals need not behave in this way. This has in turn led to the increasing interest and study of *behavioural game theory*. Closely connected to this are the reasearch areas *behavioural economics* and *behavioural finance*.

A famous example in behavioural game theory is the *ultimatum game*. The simplest version of this game is played by two players and it is a sequential game. There is a sum given, say 100 euros, that is to be divided between the two players. Player A, the leader, mentions an amount between 1 and 100 that he or she is offering to Player B. If Player B accepts, then Player B gets this amount, and Player A gets 100 minus this amount. If Player B does not accept, then both players get 0. From a purely economic perspective, it is optimal for Player A to offer Player B 1 euro. Since getting 1 is better than getting 0, Player B will accept, and Player A gets 99 euros. When this game is played in practice, however, the outcome in general differs from the "reasonable" economic one. Player B will likely perceive getting only 1 euro as very unfair and may in reality even reject to accept this if the offer is 1, despite it being economically better than 0. What an ultimatum game emphasises is the difference between pure profit optimisation and perceived fairness in negotiations. Especially in the interest of a long-term relation, the importance of mutual trust and relationship-building through communication is crucial such that agreements are perceived as win-win outcomes – in lease negotiations as well as in a lot of other business situations.

A more extreme example is the *dictator game*. In this game, the set-up is as in the ultimatum game, but now Player B has no chance of refusing to accept – the amount Player A offers to Player B is what Player B gets, and again Player A gets 100 minus this amount. Even in this case, Player A often offers Player B more than the minimum amount. While it would be economically rational for player A to keep the entire amount of 99 euro, it is hardly in the interest of a long-term relationship between both parties to impose such a distribution.

For more on the ultimatum game and the dictator game, see Chapter 3, The Ultimatum Game, in Thaler [49].

A.4   Symmetric general Cournot models

The profit maximisation condition for Firm i is given by

$$\pi_i'(q_i) = (-b)q_i + \left(a - b(q_1 + \ldots + q_n)\right) - c = 0.$$

This can be rewritten as

$$q_1 + \ldots + 2q_i + \ldots q_n = \frac{a-c}{b}. \tag{A.1}$$

Since the model is symmetric, we will have

$$q_1 = q_2 = \ldots = q_n = q,$$

where q is the common level of production for all firms. By inserting this in Equation (A.1) we get

$$nq + q = \frac{a-c}{b}.$$

The solution to this equation is given by

$$q = \frac{a-c}{b(n+1)}. \tag{A.2}$$

We note that when $n = 2$ we recover the result from Section 3.2.2 regarding the symmetric Cournot duopoly. Using the optimal quantity per firm from Equation (A.2) we get the total quantity produced

$$Q = q_1 + \ldots + q_n = nq = n\frac{a-c}{b(n+1)}.$$

The price of the good is given by

$$p = a - bQ = a - bn\frac{a-c}{b(n+1)} = a - n\frac{a-c}{n+1} = \frac{a(n+1) - an + cn}{n+1} = \frac{a+cn}{n+1}.$$

Finally, we calculate the profit for each firm, starting with

$$\pi = pq - C(q) = pq - cq = (p-c)q.$$

Now

$$p - c = \frac{a+cn}{n+1} - c = \frac{a + cn - c(n+1)}{n+1} = \frac{a-c}{n+1},$$

and we get the profit

$$\pi = \frac{a-c}{n+1} \cdot \frac{a-c}{b(n+1)} = b\left(\frac{a-c}{n+1}\right)^2.$$

A.5 Monopolistic competition

Here we derive the optimal quantities, price and profit per firm in the model of monopolistic competition from Section 3.5. Recall that the profit per firm is given by

$$\pi_i = p(q_1 + \ldots + p_n)q_i - C(q_i) = \Big(a - b(q_1 + \ldots + q_n)\Big)q_i - (cq_i + F).$$

The first order condition is

$$\pi_i'(q_i) = -bq_i + a - b(q_1 + \ldots + q_n) - c = 0.$$

It follows that $q_1 = q_2 = \ldots = q_n = q$ with

$$-bq + a - bnq - c = 0 \quad \Rightarrow \quad q = \frac{a-c}{b(n+1)},$$

and the price will be

$$p = a - bQ = a - bn\frac{a-c}{b(n+1)} = a - \frac{n(a-c)}{n+1} = \frac{a+nc}{n+1}.$$

The profit for each of the n firms is

$$\begin{aligned}\pi &= pq - (cq + F)\\ &= \frac{a+nc}{n+1} \cdot \frac{a-c}{b(n+1)} - c\frac{a-c}{b(n+1)} - F\\ &= \frac{(a-c)^2}{b(n+1)} - F.\end{aligned}$$

A.6 Concave and convex functions

A function is *concave* if the derivative is decreasing, and is *convex* if the derivative is increasing. We have the following properties of these type of functions.

Properties of concave and convex functions	
For a concave function f	For a convex function f
$f'(x)$ is decreasing	$f'(x)$ is increasing
$f''(x) \le 0$	$f''(x) \ge 0$

Note the following:

- Not every function is either concave or convex.

- The linear function $f(x) = a + bx$ is both concave *and* convex.

A.7 Approximation for certainty equivalent

The formula we want to prove is

$$CE \approx E(X) - \frac{r_A(E(X))}{2}\sigma^2(X).$$

To prove this formula, we use Taylor expansions. The starting point is the definition of the certainty equivalent,

$$E(u(X)) = u(CE),$$

and the proof is done in three steps.

(1) Expand $u(X)$ around $E(X)$:

$$u(X) \approx u(E(X)) + u'(E(X)) \cdot (X - E(X)) + \frac{1}{2}u''(E(X)) \cdot (X - E(X))^2.$$

Taking the expected value yields

$$E(u(X)) \approx u(E(X)) + 0 + \frac{1}{2}u''(E(X))\sigma^2(X) = u(E(X))\frac{1}{2}u''(E(X))\sigma^2(X).$$

(2) Expand $u(CE)$ around $E(X)$:

$$U(CE) \approx u(E(X)) + u'(E(X)) \cdot (CE - E(X)).$$

(3) Combine (1) and (2):

$$u(E(X)) + \frac{1}{2}u''(E(X))\sigma^2(X) \approx E(u(X)) = u(CE) \approx u(E(X)) + u'(E(X)) \cdot (CE - E(X)).$$

Solving for CE finally yields

$$CE \approx E(X) + \frac{1}{2} \cdot \frac{u''(E(X))}{u'(E(X))}\sigma^2(X) = E(X) - \frac{1}{2}r_A(E(X))\sigma^2(X).$$

A.8   Mathematics of the Stiglitz model

We will now prove the results from Section 7.4.2 regarding the Stiglitz model. This section follows the presentation in Perloff [43]. The value for the firm of the output of a high- and low-ability worker is w_H and w_L respectively. The fraction of high-ability employees is $0 \leq \alpha \leq 1$, and if the employer cannot distinguish between the two types, then all employees get the average salary

$$\overline{w} = \alpha w_H + (1 - \alpha)w_L.$$

In order for it to be profitable for the high-ability workers to participate in the education it must hold that

$$w_H - C \geq w_L \quad \Leftrightarrow \quad \boxed{w_H - w_L \geq C}.$$

Hence, if this condition holds, a separating equilibrium is possible. On the other hand, in a pooling equilibrium, everyone is paid the same ($= \overline{w}$) salary. If

$$w_H - C \leq \overline{w} \quad \Leftrightarrow \quad w_H - \overline{w} \leq C,$$

then it is not beneficial for a high-ability worker to get education. Hence, in this case a pooling equilibrium is possible. This last condition can be written

$$w_H - \underbrace{(\alpha w_H + (1 - \alpha)w_L)}_{=\overline{w}} < C \quad \Leftrightarrow \quad \boxed{w_H - w_L - (w_H - w_L)\alpha < C}.$$

The possible equilibria depend on the values of the parameters α and C, where $0 \leq \alpha \leq 1$ and $C \geq 0$. Now consider the two straight lines

$$C = w_H - w_L \qquad (1)$$

$$C = w_H - w_L - (w_H - w_L)\alpha. \quad (2)$$

We can conclude that:

- If $C > w_H - w_L$, then there can only be a *pooling equilibrium*.

- If $C < (w_H - w_L) \cdot (1 - \alpha)$, then there can only be a *separating equilibrium*.

The interesting part is the parameter values that allow for either a pooling or separating equilibrium to exist, as is outlined in the text in Section 7.4.2.

A.9 Calculations for the effort-depending model

Here are the the calculations for the models in Section 8.3.2. The contracter's profit is

$$s - C - c(e) = \alpha + \beta(C_0 - e + \varepsilon) - (C_0 - e + \varepsilon) - \frac{e^2}{2},$$

and the certainty equivalent of this profit is

$$
\begin{aligned}
CE(e) \quad = \quad & E\left[\alpha + \beta(C_0 - e + \varepsilon) - (C_0 - e + \varepsilon) - \frac{e^2}{2}\right] \\
& -\frac{\rho}{2}\sigma^2\left(\alpha + \beta(C_0 - e + \varepsilon) - (C_0 - e + \varepsilon) - \frac{e^2}{2}\right) \\
= \quad & \alpha + \beta(C_0 - e) - (C_0 - e) - \frac{e^2}{2} - \frac{\rho}{2}(\beta - 1)^2\sigma^2(\varepsilon) \\
= \quad & \alpha + (\beta - 1) \cdot (C_0 - e) - \frac{e^2}{2} - \frac{\rho}{2}(\beta - 1)^2\sigma_0^2.
\end{aligned}
$$

The contractor chooses the effort level such that

$$CE'(e) = 0 \quad \Leftrightarrow \quad -(\beta - 1) - e = 0 \quad \Rightarrow \quad e = 1 - \beta;$$

this is the incentive compatibility constraint. The participation contraint is $CE(e) \geq CE_0$, and again we assume that $CE_0 = 0$. The participation constraint can now be written

$$\alpha + (\beta - 1) \cdot (C_0 - e) - \frac{e^2}{2} - \frac{\rho}{2}(\beta - 1)^2\sigma_0^2 \geq 0.$$

When the contractor chooses the optimal effort level $e = 1 - \beta$, the participation constraint becomes

$$\alpha + (\beta - 1) \cdot (C_0 - (1 - \beta)) - \frac{(1 - \beta)^2}{2} - \frac{\rho}{2}(\beta - 1)^2\sigma_0^2 \geq 0$$

$$\Leftrightarrow$$

$$\alpha - C_0(1 - \beta) + (1 - \beta)^2 \cdot \frac{1 - \rho\sigma_0^2}{2} \geq 0.$$

The buyer will choose α in order for this inequality to be satisfied, and, as above, the buyer will choose the smallest α, i.e. the α making this inequality an equality:

$$\alpha = C_0(1 - \beta) - (1 - \beta)^2 \cdot \frac{1 - \rho\sigma_0^2}{2}.$$

The expected utility for the buyer is

$$E\left(v - (\alpha + \beta(C_0 - e + \varepsilon))\right) = v - (\alpha + \beta(C_0 - e)).$$

This is the expression the buyer wants to maximise. Using the expression for α from above together with $e = 1 - \beta$ results in the maximisation problem

$$\max_{\beta} v - \alpha(\beta) - \beta(C_0 - e(\beta)).$$

The first-order condition is

$$-\alpha'(\beta) - (C_0 - e(\beta)) + \beta e'(\beta) = 0.$$

Now,

$$
\begin{aligned}
\alpha'(\beta) &= -C_0 + (1 - \beta)(1 - \rho\sigma_0^2) \\
e(\beta) &= 1 - \beta \\
e'(\beta) &= -1.
\end{aligned}
$$

This results in the equation

$$C_0 - (1 - \beta) \cdot (1 - \rho\sigma_0^2) - (C_0 - (1 - \beta)) + \beta \cdot (-1) = 0,$$

with solution

$$\beta = \frac{\rho\sigma_0^2}{1 + \rho\sigma_0^2}.$$

Note that when $\rho, \sigma_0^2 > 0$, then $\beta \in (0, 1)$.

A.10 Calculations for the unkown cost model

We want to find

$$\max_{c_H, c_L} v - \alpha\big((1 + r)c_H + rT_H + g(\beta_H - c_H)\big) - (1 - \alpha)\big((1 + r)c_L + rT_L + g(\beta_L - c_L)\big)$$

subject to the following two equality constraints:

$$
\begin{aligned}
T_L &= g(\beta_L - c_L) \\
T_H &= g(\beta_H - c_H) + g(\beta_L - c_L) - g(\beta_H - c_L),
\end{aligned}
$$

where $g(e) = e^2/2$. Replacing T_L and T_H from the constraints into the function we want to maximise results in the two first-order conditions with respect to c_H and c_L respectively:

$$
\begin{aligned}
-\alpha\big((1 + r) - r(\beta_H - c_H) - (\beta_H - c_H)\big) &= 0 \\
-\alpha r\big(-(\beta_L - c_L) + \beta_H - c_L\big) - (1 - \alpha)\big((1 + r) - r(\beta_L - c_L) - (\beta_L - c_L)\big) &= 0
\end{aligned}
$$

These two equations can be written

$$
\begin{aligned}
\beta_H - c_H &= 1 \\
\beta_L - c_L &= 1 - \frac{r}{1 + r} \cdot \frac{\alpha}{1 - \alpha} \cdot (\beta_L - \beta_H);
\end{aligned}
$$

which are the two equations on page 125.

A.11   Calculations without vertical integration

When the cost for the manufacturer of producing Q units of the good is

$$C(Q) = c \cdot Q,$$

and it charges the retailer $p_r \cdot Q$ for Q units of the good, then the cost function for the retailer is

$$C_r(Q) = p_r \cdot Q.$$

If both the producer and the retailer are monopolists, then they compete in a Stackelberg game, where the producer first sets the price p_r that the retailer has to pay, and then the retailer sets the price p paid by the consumers. We further assume that the consumers' demand function for the product sold by the retailer is given by

$$Q = 1 - p.$$

To solve this type of game, we start, as always, at the end, i.e. we start with the retailer.

The retailer

In this case the inverse demand function is given by the linear function $p = 1 - Q$, and as is shown in Section 1.4.2, this results in the marginal revenue

$$MR = 1 - 2Q.$$

The marginal cost for the retailer is given by

$$MC = C_r'(Q) = p_r,$$

so we have

$$MR = MC \quad \Leftrightarrow \quad 1 - 2Q = p_r \quad \Rightarrow \quad Q = \frac{1 - p_r}{2},$$

where Q is the quantity the retailer sells to the consumers. Hence, the price to the consumers is

$$p = 1 - Q = 1 - \frac{1 - p_r}{2} = \frac{1 + p_r}{2}.$$

The profit for the retailer is

$$\pi_r = pQ_r - C_r(Q_r) = \frac{1 + p_r}{2} \cdot \frac{1 - p_r}{2} - p_r \cdot \frac{1 - p_r}{2} = \left(\frac{1 + p_r}{2} \right)^2.$$

The producer

Given the price p_r, the quantity

$$Q = \frac{1 - p_r}{2}$$

will be sold by the retailer, and this is also the amount the retailer wants to buy from the producer. Hence, this is the retailer's demand function. Solving for p_r we get the retailer's inverse demand function:

$$p_r = 1 - 2Q.$$

The producer's maximisation problem is $MR = MC$. If we let Q_r denote the quantity that the producer sells to the retailer, then

$$MR = 1 - 4Q_r \quad \text{and} \quad MC = C'(Q_r) = c.$$

This gives

$$MR = MC \iff 1 - 4Q_r = c \implies Q_r = \frac{1-c}{4}.$$

This results in the price

$$p_r = 1 - 2Q_r = 1 - 2 \cdot \frac{1-c}{4} = \frac{1+c}{2}$$

that the producer charges the retailer, and the price

$$p = \frac{1 + p_r}{2} = \frac{1 + \frac{1+c}{2}}{2} = \frac{3+c}{4}$$

that the retailer charges the customers. The retailer's profit is

$$\pi_r = \left(\frac{1 - \frac{1+c}{2}}{2}\right)^2 = \left(\frac{\frac{1}{2} - \frac{c}{2}}{2}\right)^2 = \frac{(1-c)^2}{16},$$

and the producer's profit is

$$\pi_p = p_r Q_r - c Q_r = \frac{1+c}{2} \cdot \frac{1-c}{4} - c \cdot \frac{1-c}{4} = \frac{(1-c)^2}{8}$$

This results in the total profit

$$\pi_r + \pi_p = \frac{3(1-c)^2}{16}.$$

Solutions to the exercises

Chapter 1

1.1 a) If we fix the utility level to $\overline{U}$, then an indifference curve is given by

$$\overline{U} = x_1 + x_2 \quad \Leftrightarrow \quad x_2 = \overline{U} - x_1.$$

Hence, an indifference curve is a straight line in the x_1-x_2-plane with slope -1.

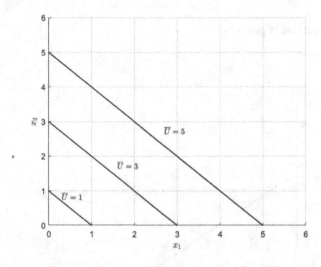

b) In the case of a linear utility function, the solution will be a corner solution, i.e. the individual will consume zero of one good, and put the whole income in buying the other good. Since $U(x_1, x_2) = x_1 + x_2$, the utility is equal to the sum of the consumed goods and the apartment buyer will choose to only consume the cheaper good. Since $p_2 = 2p_1$, this is good 1. It follows that the apartment buyer will find an apartment as close as possible to the city centre.

1.2 a) If we fix the utility level to $\overline{U}$, then an indifference curve is given by

$$\overline{U} = \max(x_1, x_2).$$

This results in indifference curves of the following type:

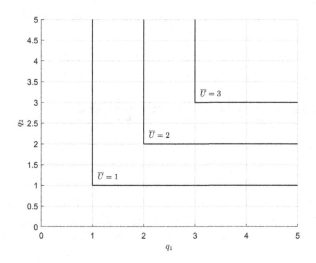

b) The budget line is given by

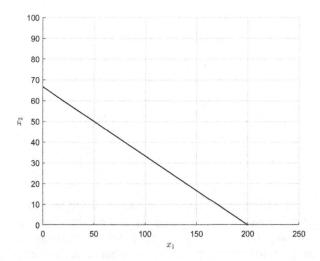

c) Due to how the indifference curves look, the optimal quantities will be at a point where $x_1 = x_2$. In this case, that is when $x_1 = x_2 = 50$, as is shown in the following graph.

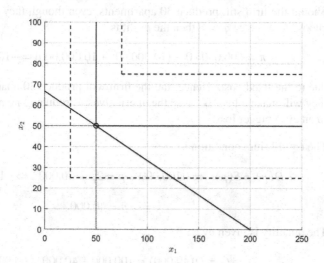

d) We get the demand function by inserting the optimal quantities in the equation for the budget line. In this case $x_1 = x_2$, so we get

$$p_1 x_1 + p_2 x_2 = m \iff p_1 x_1 + p_2 x_1 = m \implies x_1 = \frac{m}{p_1 + p_2}.$$

1.3 The first order condition is
$$p = MC.$$

In this case
$$MC(q) = C'(q) = 20{,}000q.$$

a) When $p = 1{,}800{,}000$ we get the equation
$$1{,}800{,}000 = 20{,}000q \implies q = \frac{1{,}800{,}000}{20{,}000} = 90.$$

The profit is
$$\begin{aligned} \pi &= p \cdot q - C(q) \\ &= 1{,}800{,}000 \cdot 90 - \left(10{,}000 \cdot 90^2 + 10{,}000{,}000\right) \\ &= 71{,}000{,}000{,}000 > 0, \end{aligned}$$

so the firm will produce 90 apartments.

b) When $p = 600{,}000$ we get the equation
$$600{,}000 = 20{,}000q \implies q = \frac{600{,}000}{20{,}000} = 30.$$

The profit is
$$\begin{aligned} \pi &= p \cdot q - C(q) \\ &= 600{,}000 \cdot 30 - \left(10{,}000 \cdot 30^2 + 10{,}000{,}000\right) \\ &= -1{,}000{,}000 < 0. \end{aligned}$$

Should the firm still produce 30 apartments, even though they make a loss? If they choose to produce $q = 0$, then the profit is

$$\pi = 600{,}000 \cdot 0 - \left(10{,}000 \cdot 0^2 + 10{,}000{,}000\right) = -10{,}000{,}000$$

due to the fixed cost. Hence, the the firm will produce 30 apartments, even though they will make a loss, because the alternative of producing no apartments will result in an even bigger loss.

1.4   a) The equilibrium condition is

$$D(p) = S(p) \quad \Leftrightarrow \quad 100{,}000 - p = 2p - 20{,}000 \quad \Leftrightarrow \quad 120{,}000 = 3p$$

$$\Rightarrow \quad p = 40{,}000.$$

The quantity is given by

$$Q = D(40{,}000) = 100{,}000 - 40{,}000 = 60{,}000.$$

We can also use the supply function:

$$Q = S(40{,}000) = 2 \cdot 40{,}000 - 20{,}000 = 60{,}000.$$

b) $CS = 1{,}800{,}000{,}000$ and $PS = 900{,}000{,}000$.

c) The equilibrium condition is

$$D(p) = S(p) \quad \Leftrightarrow \quad \frac{120{,}000}{p} = 30{,}000p \quad \Leftrightarrow \quad 120{,}000 = 30{,}000p^2.$$

This equation can be written

$$p^2 = \frac{120{,}000}{30{,}000} = 4 \quad \Rightarrow \quad p = 2.$$

The quantity is given by

$$Q = D(2) = \frac{120{,}000}{2} = 60{,}000.$$

Using the supply functions gives the same result:

$$Q = S(2) = 30{,}000 \cdot 2 = 60{,}000.$$

1.5   a) The equilibrium condition is

$$D(p) = S(p) \Leftrightarrow 1{,}950{,}000 - p = p \Leftrightarrow 1{,}950{,}000 = 2p \Rightarrow p = \frac{1{,}950{,}000}{2} = 975{,}0$$

b) The interest rate r satisfies

$$975{,}000 = \frac{1{,}000{,}000}{1 + r} \quad \Leftrightarrow \quad 1 + r = \frac{1{,}000{,}000}{975{,}000} \approx 1.0256 \quad \Rightarrow \quad r \approx 0.0256.$$

1.6 Each firm sets it price according to

$$p = MC \iff p = C'(q) = 0.02q \implies q = \frac{p}{0.02} = 50p.$$

Hence, the total quantity produced is

$$Q = \sum_{i=1}^{12} q_i = 12q = 12 \cdot 50p = 600p$$

This is also the supply function:

$$S(p) = 600p.$$

In equilibrium

$$D(p) = S(p) \iff 50{,}000 - 1{,}900p = 600p \iff 50{,}000 = 2{,}500p \implies p = \frac{50{,}000}{2{,}500} = 20.$$

1.7 a) The maximisation condition for the monopolist is

$$MR = MC.$$

In this case

$$MR(Q) = 10 - 4Q$$

and

$$MC(Q) = C'(Q) = 2.$$

Hence, the number of hotels the real estate investor builds satisfies

$$MR = MC \iff 10 - 4Q = 2 \iff 8 = 4Q \implies Q = 2.$$

The price will be

$$p = 10 - 2Q = 10 - 2 \cdot 2 = 6,$$

and the profit is

$$\pi = p \cdot Q - C(Q) = 6 \cdot 2 - 2 \cdot 2 = 8.$$

b) Since we still have

$$MC(Q) = C'(Q) = 2,$$

the condition $MR = MC$ again results in $Q = 2$. But in this case the fixed cost can influence the investment choise. The price when $Q = 2$ is given by

$$p = 10 - 2 \cdot 2 = 6,$$

and the profit is

$$\pi = p \cdot Q - C(Q) = 6 \cdot 2 - (2 \cdot 2 + F) = 8 - F.$$

Hence, as long as $F \leq 8$, the profit satisfies $\pi \geq 0$, and $Q = 2$ hotels are built. But if $F > 0$, then the profit is negative, and $Q = 0$ hotels are built in this case.

1.8 a) The rent at which demand is equal to zero is given by

$$D(p) = 0 \iff 10{,}000 - 2p = 0 \iff 10{,}000 = 2p \implies p = 5{,}000.$$

b) The equilibrium condition is

$$D(p) = S(p) \iff 10{,}000 - 2p = 6p \iff 10{,}000 = 8p \implies p = \frac{10{,}000}{8} = 1{,}250,$$

which will be the monthly rent. The number of apartments that are built is

$$Q = D(1{,}250) = 10{,}000 - 2 \cdot 1{,}250 = 7{,}500.$$

c) If the rent is regulated, then this is the maximum rent that a landlord is allowed to charge. Since the market rent would be €1,250 > €1,000, there will only be built

$$Q = S(1{,}000) = 6 \cdot 1{,}000 = 6{,}000$$

apartments. The situation is depicted in the following figure.

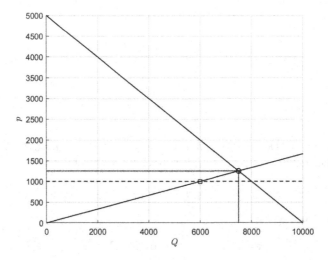

d) The deadweight loss in this case is equal to the area of the triangle with corners in ∘, □ and ∗.

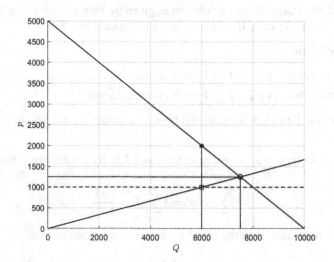

This area is given by

$$\text{DWL} = \frac{(2,000 - 1,000) \cdot (7,500 - 6,000)}{2} = 750,000.$$

Chapter 2

2.1 a) The best responses for each of the players is as follows:

- Player A chooses Strategy I → Player B chooses Strategy II

- Player A chooses Strategy II → Player B chooses Strategy II

- Player B chooses Strategy I → Player A chooses Strategy II

- Player B chooses Strategy II → Player A chooses Strategy I

b) There is one Nash equilibrium: Player A choosing Strategy I and Player B choosing Strategy II. This is the only choice of strategies from which none of the players wants to deviate.

2.2 We have the following best responses:

- Player A chooses Strategy I → Player B chooses Strategy I

- Player A chooses Strategy II → Player B chooses Strategy II

- Player B chooses Strategy I → Player A chooses Strategy II

- Player B chooses Strategy II → Player A chooses Strategy II

We see that the unique Nash equilibrium is given by Player A choosing Strategy II and Player B choosing Strategy II, and the payoffs is this case are $(5, 3)$.

2.3 We start with Firm B:

- If Firm A chooses $q_A = 1 \rightarrow$ Firm B chooses $q_B = 2$.
- If Firm A chooses $q_A = 3 \rightarrow$ Firm B chooses $q_B = 3$.

This is known to Firm A, who then will choose to produce $q_A = 1$, resulting in the payofffs $(3, 8)$.

2.4 We use the same type of argument as in Section 2.3.3. By not deviating, the value for each player is

$$\sum_{t=1}^{\infty} 3 \cdot \delta^t = 3 \sum_{t=1}^{\infty} \delta^t = \frac{3\delta}{1-\delta}.$$

If one of them deviates, then the payoff to the deviating player is

$$5 \cdot \delta + \sum_{t=2}^{\infty} 0 \cdot \delta^t = 5\delta.$$

The cooperative strategy is viable if

$$\frac{3\delta}{1-\delta} \geq 5\delta \iff 3 \geq 5(1-\delta) \iff \frac{3}{5} \geq 1-\delta \implies \delta \geq 1 - \frac{3}{5} = 2/5 = 0.4.$$

Chapter 3

3.1 a) This situation is a symmetric Cournot duopoly. We know from Section 3.2.2 that with a constant marginal cost c and a linear inverted demand function $p = a - bQ$, the optimal quantities are given by

$$q_1 = q_2 = \frac{a-c}{b}.$$

In our case we have

$$a = 10, \ b = 1 \ \text{and} \ c = 3.$$

This results in the optimal quantities

$$q_1 = q_2 = \frac{10-3}{3} = \frac{7}{3} \approx 2.33.$$

b) When the two firms form a cartel, they work as a monopoly on the market. This monopoly wants to produce the quantity Q such that $MR = MC$:

$$MR(Q) = MC(Q) \iff 10 - 2Q = 3 \iff 7 = 2Q \implies Q = \frac{7}{2} = 3.5.$$

c) Now, $MC(q) = C'(q) = 4$. For the oligopoly model, we get the new quantities

$$q_1 = q_2 = \frac{10-4}{3} = 2,$$

and for the cartel the optimal quantity is

$$Q = \frac{10-4}{2} = 3.$$

3.2 This is an example of an asymmetric Cournot duopoly. Firm 1 wants to solve

$$\max_{q_1} p(Q)q_1 - C_1(q_1) = \max_{q_1} \left(10 - (q_1 + q_2)\right)q_1 - 2q_1.$$

The first-order condition is

$$10 - (q_1 + q_2) - q_1 - 2 = 0 \iff 8 - q_2 = 2q_1 \implies q_1 = 4 - \frac{q_2}{2}.$$

This is Firm 1's reaction function. Firm 2 wants to solve

$$\max_{q_2} p(Q)q_2 - C_2(q_2) = \max_{q_2} \left(10 - (q_1 + q_2)\right)q_2 - 4q_2.$$

The first-order condition is

$$10 - (q_1 + q_2) - q_2 - 4 = 0 \iff 6 - q_1 = 2q_2 \implies q_2 = 3 - \frac{q_1}{2},$$

which is Firm 2's reaction function. The equilibrium is found when

$$\begin{cases} q_1 & = & 4 - \dfrac{q_2}{2} \\ \\ q_2 & = & 3 - \dfrac{q_1}{2}. \end{cases}$$

The solution to this system of equations is

$$q_1 = \frac{10}{3} \approx 3.33 \text{ and } q_2 = \frac{4}{3} \approx 1.33.$$

3.3 The equation

$$q_1 + \ldots + 2q_i + \ldots + q_n = \frac{a - c}{b}$$

can be written

$$q_i = \frac{a - c}{b} - q_1 - \ldots - q_i - \ldots - q_n = \frac{a - c}{b} - Q.$$

Since the right-hand side is independent of i, this shows that $q_1 = q_2 = \ldots = q_n$.

3.4 This is an example of an asymmetric Cournot duopoly. Firm 1 wants to solve

$$\max_{q_1} p_1(q_1, q_2)q_1 - C(q_1) = \max_{q_1}(10 - q_1 - q_2)q_1 - 4q_1.$$

The first-order condition is

$$10 - q_1 - q_2 - q_1 - 4 = 0 \iff 6 - q_2 = 2q_1 \implies q_1 = 3 - \frac{q_2}{2},$$

which is Firm 1's reaction function. Firm 2 wants to solve

$$\max_{q_2} p_2(q_1, q_2)q_2 - C(q_2) = \max_{q_2} \left(18 - 2q_1 - 2q_2\right)q_2 - 4q_2.$$

The first-order condition is

$$18 - 2q_1 - 2q_2 - 2q_2 - 4 = 0 \iff 14 - 2q_1 = 4q_2 \implies q_2 = 3.5 - \frac{q_1}{2},$$

which is Firm 2's reaction function. The equilibrium is found when

$$\begin{cases} q_1 &=& 3 - \dfrac{q_2}{2} \\[3mm] q_2 &=& 3.5 - \dfrac{q_1}{2}. \end{cases}$$

The solution to this system of equations is

$$q_1 = \frac{5}{3} \approx 1.67 \text{ and } q_2 = \frac{8}{3} \approx 2.67.$$

3.5 Firm 1 wants to solve

$$\max_{p_1} p_1 D_1(p_1, p_2) - C(D_1(p_1, p_2)) = \max_{p_1} p_1(10 - p_1 + 2p_2) - (10 - p_1 + 2p_2).$$

The first-order condition is

$$10 - p_1 + 2p_2 - p_1 + 1 = 0 \iff 11 + 2p_2 = 2p_1 \implies p_1 = 5.5 + p_2,$$

which is Firm 1's reaction function. Firm 2 wants to solve

$$\max_{p_2} p_2 D_1(p_1, p_2) - C(D_2(p_1, p_2)) = \max_{p_2} p_2(5 + p_1 - p_2) - (5 + p_1 - p_2).$$

The first-order condition is

$$5 + p_1 - p_2 - p_2 + 1 = 0 \iff 6 + p_1 = 2p_2 \implies p_2 = 3 + \frac{p_1}{2},$$

which is Firm 1's reaction function. The equilibrium is found when

$$\begin{cases} p_1 &=& 5.5 + p_2 \\[3mm] p_2 &=& 3 + \dfrac{p_1}{2}. \end{cases}$$

The solution to this system of equations is

$$p_1 = 17 \text{ and } p_2 = 11.5.$$

It follows that

$$q_1 = D_1(17, 11.5) = 10 - 17 + 2 \cdot 11.5 = 16$$

and

$$q_2 = D_2(17, 11.5) = 5 + 17 - 11.5 = 10.5.$$

3.6 We use the methodology from Section 3.5. It follows that the number of firms in equilibrium is given by

$$n = \frac{a - c}{\sqrt{bF}} - 1,$$

where in our case we have

$$a = 25, \ b = 2, \ c = 5 \text{ and } F = 8.$$

This gives

$$n = \frac{25 - 5}{\sqrt{2 \cdot 8}} - 1 = 4.$$

Chapter 4

4.1 a) Any equilibrium point satisfies

$$\begin{cases} a_1 &= R_1(a_2) \\ a_2 &= R_2(a_1). \end{cases}$$

In this case the system of equations is

$$\begin{cases} a_1 &= a_2^2 \\ a_2 &= \dfrac{a_1 + 1}{2}. \end{cases}$$

Inserting the first equation in the second gives

$$a_2 = \frac{a_2^2 + 1}{2} \iff 2a_2 = a_2^2 + 1 \iff a_2^2 - 2a_2 + 1 = 0 \implies a_2 = 1.$$

Using this in the first equation gives $a_1 = 1^2 = 1$.

b) Since

$$R_1'(a_2) = 2a_2 \geq 0$$

and

$$R_2'(a_1) = \frac{1}{2} > 0,$$

we can conclude that the actions are strategic complements.

4.2 See the box "Overview: Market entry scenarios" on page 70.

4.3 See the box "Tough and soft firms" on page 71.

4.4 In both the case of the Top dog and Fat cat strategies, the incumbent firm overinvest, while in the case of the Lean and hungry look and the Puppy dog strategy, the incumbent firm underinvests.

Chapter 5

5.1 a) The expected value is given by

$$E(X) = 1{,}000{,}000 \cdot 0.2 + 0 \cdot 0.5 + (-500{,}000) \cdot 0.3 = 50{,}000.$$

b) The variance is given by

$$\begin{aligned} \sigma^2(X) &= (1{,}000{,}000 - 50{,}000)^2 \cdot 0.2 \\ &\quad + (0 - 50{,}000)^2 \cdot 0.5 \\ &\quad + (-500{,}000 - 50{,}000)^2 \cdot 0.3 \\ &= 272{,}500{,}000{,}000. \end{aligned}$$

c) The expected utility is given by

$$
\begin{aligned}
E(u(X)) &= u(1{,}000{,}000) \cdot 0.2 + u(0) \cdot 0.5 + u(-500{,}000) \cdot 0.3 \\
&= \ln(1{,}000{,}000 + 800{,}000) \cdot 0.2 \\
&\quad + \ln(0 + 800{,}000) \cdot 0.5 \\
&\quad + \ln(-500{,}000 + 800{,}000) \cdot 0.2 \\
&\approx 13.46.
\end{aligned}
$$

d) The certainty equivalent CE is the constant satisfying

$$
u(CE) = E(u(X))
$$

$$
\Leftrightarrow
$$

$$
\ln(CE + 800{,}000) \approx 13.46 \quad \Leftrightarrow \quad CE + 800{,}000 \approx 701{,}029 \quad \Rightarrow \quad CE \approx -98{,}971.
$$

e) Since the certainty equivalent is negative, the investment should not be done.

5.2 Since

$$
u'(x) = \frac{1}{2\sqrt{x}} \quad \text{and} \quad u''(x) = -\frac{1}{4}x^{-3/2},
$$

we get

$$
r_A(x) = -\frac{u''(x)}{u'(x)} = -\frac{-\frac{1}{4}x^{-3/2}}{\frac{1}{2\sqrt{x}}} = \frac{1}{2x}.
$$

5.3 a) In this case we can use the exact formula

$$
CE = E(X) - \frac{r_A}{2}\sigma^2 = 300 - \frac{2}{2} \cdot 10^2 = 200.
$$

b) We see from the formula

$$
CE = E(X) - \frac{r_A}{2}\sigma^2
$$

that the higher the risk aversion, measured by r_A, the lower is the certainty equivalent.

5.4 The definition of the zero utility premium Π is that it satisfies

$$
E\left[u(Y)\right] = E\left[u(Y + \Pi - Z)\right].
$$

With $Y = y$ a constant, this simplifies to

$$
u(y) = E\left[u(y + \Pi - Z)\right].
$$

When

$$
u(x) = -e^{-ax} \quad \text{for a constant } a > 0,
$$

the defining equation is

$$
-e^{-ay} = E\left(-e^{-a(y+\Pi-Z)}\right) = -e^{-a(y+\Pi)}E\left(e^{aZ}\right)
$$

$$
\Leftrightarrow
$$

$$
1 = e^{-a\Pi}E\left(e^{aZ}\right)
$$

$$
\Leftrightarrow
$$

$$
e^{a\Pi} = E\left(e^{aZ}\right)
$$

$$
\Leftrightarrow
$$

$$
a\Pi = \ln\left(E\left(e^{aZ}\right)\right) \quad \Rightarrow \quad \Pi = \frac{1}{a}\ln\left(E\left(e^{aZ}\right)\right).
$$

Chapter 6

6.1 In a complete contract not everything is observable to everyone, but what's observable is also verifiable. In an incomplete contract, the observable information is not verifiable.

6.2 The principal-agent relationship does not take the cost of writing a contract into account.

6.3 According to Oliver Hart, a firm arises in situations where it is not possible to write good contracts. Here a "good contract" is a complete contract, so the fact that contracts are incomplete results in the existence of firms.

Chapter 7

7.1 In screening, the uninformed party wants information from the informed party, while in signalling, the informed party wants to inform the uninformed party.

7.2 In the case of asymmetric information, which is the case in which there can be adverse selection, the expected value of a property for the (uninformed) buyers is

$$300 \cdot \alpha + 600 \cdot (1 - \alpha) = 600 - 300\alpha.$$

If this value is higher than the value 500 that the (informed) seller of a property that is well maintained wants to sell it for, then all properties will be sold. This condition is

$$600 - 300\alpha \geq 500 \quad \Leftrightarrow \quad 100 \geq 300\alpha \quad \Rightarrow \quad \alpha \leq \frac{1}{3} \approx 0.33.$$

7.3   a) For a low-ability worker, the payoffs from the two wage schemes are as follows:

$$\text{Wage scheme I:} \quad 10w$$
$$\text{Wage scheme II:} \quad w_H + 9w_L$$

In order for the low-ability workers not to choose wage scheme II, it must hold that

$$w_H + 9w_L < 10w.$$

   b) When $w_L = 0.9$, $w = 1$ and $w_H = 2$, then we have the following total wages for the two different groups:

	High-ability worker	Low-ability worker
Wage scheme I	$10w = 10$	$10w = 10$
Wage scheme II	$10w_H = 20$	$w_H + 9w_L = 10.1$

Hence, both groups will choose wage scheme II. This will probably lead the high-ability workers to quit, and the result of this pooling equilibrium is adverse selection (only low-ability workers continue to work).

7.4   a) In this case the good is the level of renovation L, and the bad is the rent R. We see that for a fixed utility level $\overline{U}$, the slope of an indifference curve for Group 2 is steeper than an indifference curve for Group 1, so Group 2 will prefer a low rent to a renovated apartment more than Group 1.

   b) We get the following utilities for the two groups:

	Utility for Group 1	Utility for Group 2
Contract I	$2 - 2 \cdot 1^2 = 0$	$3 \cdot 2 - 6 \cdot 1^3 = 0$
Contract II	$4 - 2 \cdot 2^2 = -4$	$3 \cdot 4 - 6 \cdot 2^3 = -36$

Hence, both groups will choose Contract I, and the resulting equilibrium is a pooling one. This may lead to tenants in Group 1 moving elsewhere in order to get a higher level of renovation.

c) We get the following utilities for the two groups:

	Utility for Group 1	Utility for Group 2
Contract I	$2 - 2 \cdot 1^2 = 0$	$3 \cdot 2 - 6 \cdot 1^3 = 0$
Contract II	$5 - 2 \cdot 1.5^2 = 0.5$	$3 \cdot 5 - 6 \cdot 1.5^3 = -5.25$

In this case Group 1 will choose Contract II, and Group II will choose Contract I, so in this case we get a screening equilibrium.

Chapter 8

8.1   a) The company wants the project manager to put down the effort that maximises the profit

$$\pi(e) = 5e - e^2 - w(e) = 5e - e^2 - e = 4e - e^2.$$

The first-order condition is

$$\pi'(e) = 0 \iff 4 - 2e = 0 \implies e = 2.$$

Hence, the company wants the project manager to put down the effort $e = 2$.

b) The project manager wants to maximise his or her payoff

$$w(e) - c(e) = e - e^2/2.$$

The first-order condition is

$$1 - e = 0 \implies e = 1,$$

so the project manager wants to put down the effort $e = 1$.

c) In this case the project manager wants to maximise

$$w(e) - c(q) = \alpha + \beta e - \frac{e^2}{2}.$$

The first-order condition is

$$\beta - e = 0 \implies e = \beta.$$

d) With the choice $e = \beta$, the payoff to the project manager is

$$\alpha + \beta \cdot \beta - \frac{\beta^2}{2} = \alpha + \frac{\beta^2}{2}.$$

When $w(e) = e$, we know from b) that the project manager chooses $e = 1$. With this choice the payoff is

$$1 - \frac{1^2}{2} = \frac{1}{2}.$$

In order for the project manager to accept the new salary contract, the company must offer a contract that satisfies

$$\alpha + \frac{\beta^2}{2} \geq \frac{1}{2}.$$

e) To determine the company's profit, we first of all use that $e = \beta$. The participation constraint from d) is satisfied if it is an equality, and this is what we will use when determining in the company's profit:

$$\begin{aligned}
\pi(\beta) &= 5\beta - \beta^2 - (\alpha + \beta \cdot \beta) \\
&= 5\beta - \beta^2 - \left(\frac{1}{2} - \frac{\beta^2}{2} + \beta^2 \right) \\
&= 5\beta - \frac{3\beta^2}{2} - \frac{1}{2}.
\end{aligned}$$

The first-order condition is

$$\pi'(\beta) = 0 \iff 5 - 3\beta = 0 \implies \beta = \frac{5}{3}.$$

This is the optimal value of β.

f) To find the optimal α we use the participation constraint:

$$\alpha = \frac{1}{2} - \frac{\beta^2}{2} = \frac{1}{2} - \frac{1}{2} \cdot \frac{5^2}{3^2} = -\frac{8}{9}.$$

8.2 We have

$$Y = w(q) - c(e) = 1 + 2q - 3e^2 = 1 + 2(3e + X) - 3e^2 = 1 + 6e - 3e^2 + 2X.$$

a) In this case, the employee values the random payoff as

$$\begin{aligned}
E(Y) - \sigma^2(Y) &= E(1 + 6e - 3e^2 + 2X) - \sigma^2(1 + 6e - 3e^2 + 2X) \\
&= 1 + 6e - 3e^2 + 2E(X) - 4\sigma^2(X) \\
&= 1 + 6e - 3e^2 + 2 \cdot 0 - 4 \cdot 4 \\
&= -15 + 6e - 3e^2.
\end{aligned}$$

The first-order condition is

$$6 - 6e = 0 \implies e = 1.$$

In this case the utility of putting down this effort is given by

$$-15 + 6 \cdot 1 - 3 \cdot 1^2 = -12 < 0 = CE_0.$$

Hence, the employee is better off not accepting to work, so he or she will not put down this effort, and will instead choose to leave the employment.

b) When the employee is risk neutral, than he or she values the random payoff Y as $E(Y)$. We get

$$E(Y) = E(1 + 6e - 3e^2 + 2X) = 1 + 6e - 3e^2 + 2E(X) = 1 + 6e - 3e^2.$$

The first-order condition is

$$6 - 6e = 0 \implies e = 1.$$

In this case the utility of putting down this effort is given by

$$1 + 6 \cdot 1 - 3 \cdot 1^2 = 4 > 0 = CE_0,$$

so the employee will put down the effort $e = 1$.

Chapter 9

9.1 There are two subgames, which are circled in the following figure.

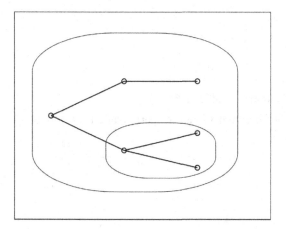

9.2 When $k = 60$ the payoff to the construction company when the property developer wants to renegotiate the contract is $25 - 60/2 = -5 < 0$, so the payoffs in the subgame perfect Nash equilibrium are $(0, 0)$.

When $k = 20$ the payoff to the construction company when the property developer wants to renegotiate the contract is $25 - 20/2 = 15 > 0$, so the payoffs in the subgame perfect Nash equilibrium are $(15, 35)$

9.3 In this case the payoffs are given by

$$
\begin{aligned}
\text{Constructor's payoff} &= 25 - \frac{k - 10}{2} = 30 - \frac{k}{2} \\
\text{Developer's payoff} &= 25 - \frac{10 - k}{2} = 20 + \frac{k}{2}
\end{aligned}
$$

as functions of the sunk cost k. In order for the constructor to accept to enter into the project, it must hold that

$$0 \leq \text{Constructor's payoff} = 30 - \frac{k}{2} \iff \frac{k}{2} \leq 30 \implies k \leq 60,$$

which are the values of k for which the project is being realised.

Bibliography

[1] Akerlof, G. A. (1970), 'The market for lemons: Quality uncertainty and the market mechanism', *Quaterly Journal of Economics*, Vol. 84, pp. 488–500.

[2] Atkin, B. & Brooks, A. (2015), 'Total facility management', *John Wiley & Sons, Inc.*

[3] Baum, A., Crosby, N., Gallimore, P., McAllister, P. & Gray, A. (2000), 'The influence of valuers and valuations on the workings of the commercial property investment market', *Royal Institution of Chartered Surveyors/Investment Property Forum*.

[4] Ben-Shahar, D. (2004), 'Productive Signaling Equilibria and Over-Maintenance: An Application to Real Estate Markets', *Journal of Real Estate Finance and Economics*, Vol. 28, No. 2/3, pp. 255–271.

[5] Bolton, P. & Dewatripont, M. (2005), 'Contract theory', *The MIT Press*.

[6] Bulow, J. I., Geanakopols, J. D. & Klemperer, P. D. (1985), 'Multimarket Oligopoly: Strategic Substitutes and Complements', *Journal of Political Economy*, Vol. 93, No. 3, pp. 488–511.

[7] Ceric, A. (2014), 'Strategies for minimizing information asymmetries in construction projects: project managers' perceptions', *Journal of Business Economics and Management*, Vol. 15, No. 3, pp. 424–440.

[8] Coase, R. H. (1937), 'The Nature of the Firm', *Economica*, Vol. 4, No. 16, pp. 386–405.

[9] Coase, R. H. (1960), 'The Problem of Social Cost', *The Journal of Law & Economics*, Vol. 3, pp. 1–44.

[10] DeCanio, S. J. & Fremstad, A. (2013), 'Game theory and climate diplomacy', *Ecological Economics*, Vol. 85, pp. 177–178. https://doi.org/10.1016/j.ecolecon.2011.04.016.

[11] Dixit, A. K. & Nalebuff, B. J. (2008), 'The Art of Strategy: A Game Theorist's Guide to Success in Business and Life', *W. W. Norton*.

[12] Dixit, A. K., Skeath, S. & McAdams, D. (2021), 'Games of Strategy', 5th Ed., *W. W. Norton*.

[13] Eriksen, M. D., Fout, H. B., Palim, M. & Rosenblatt, E. (2020), 'Contract Price Confirmation Bias: Evidence from Repeat Appraisals', *The Journal of Real Estate Finance and Economics*, Vol. 60, pp. 77–98.

[14] Eriksson, P. E., Atkin, B. and Nilsson, T. (2009), 'Overcoming barriers to partnering through cooperative procurement procedures', *Engineering, Construction and Architectural Management*, Vol. 16, No. 6, pp. 598–611.

[15] Fudenberg, D. & Tirole, J. (1984), 'The Fat-Cat Effect, The Puppy-Dog Ploy, and the Lean and Hungry Look', *The American Economic Review*, Vol. 74, No. 2, pp. 361–366.

[16] Gibbons, R. (1992), 'Game theory for applied economists', *Princeton University Press*.

[17] Gravelle, H. & Rees, R. (2004), 'Microeconomics', 3rd Ed., *Prentice Hall*.

[18] Grossman, S. J. & Hart, O. D. (1986), 'The costs and benefits of ownership: A theory of vertical and lateral integration', *Journal of Political Economy*, Vol. 94, No. 4, pp. 691–719.

[19] Hart, O. (1989), 'An Economict's Perspective on the Theory of the Firm', *Columbia Law Review*, Vol. 89, No. 7, pp. 1757–1774.

[20] Hart, O. (1995), 'Firms, Contracts, and Financial Structure', *Oxford University Press*.

[21] Hart, O. & Holmström, B. (1987), 'The Theory of Contracts', *Advances in Economic Theory, Fifth World Congress*, Ed. T. R. Bewley, pp. 71–155.

[22] Hendrikse, G. (2003), 'Economics and Management of Organizations: Co-ordination, Motivation and Strategy', *McGraw-Hill*.

[23] Holmström, B. & Roberts, J. (1998), 'The Boundaries of the Firm Revisited', *Journal of Economic Perspectives*, Vol. 12, No. 4, pp. 73–94.

[24] Jensen, M. C. & Meckling, W. H. (1976), 'Theory of the firm: Managerial behavior, agency costs and ownership structure', *Journal of Financial Economics*, Vol. 3, No. 4, pp. 305–360.

[25] Kadefors, A. & Bröchner, J. (2004), 'Building users, owners and service providers: new relations and their effects', *Facilities*, Vol. 22, No. 11/12, pp. 278–283. https://doi.org/10.1108/02632770410561268.

[26] Kahkonen, K. (2015), 'Role and nature of systemic innovations in construction and real estate sector', *Construction Innovation*, Vol. 15, No. 2, pp. 130–133. https://doi.org/10.1108/CI-12-2014-0055.

[27] Kamalahasan, A. (2013), 'Client influence on property valuation: A literature review', *International Journal of Real Estate Studies*, Vol. 8, No. 2.

[28] Kay, J. & King, M. (2020), 'Radical Uncertainty', *The Bridge Street Press*.

[29] Kuhn, H. W. & Nasar, S. (eds.) (2002), 'The essential John Nash', *Princeton University Press*.

[30] Laffont, J.-J. & Tirole, J. (1993), 'A Theory of Incentives in Procurement and Regulation', *The MIT Press*.

[31] Lazear, E. P. (1999), 'Personnel Economics: Past Lessons and Future Directions', *Journal of Labor Economics*, Vol. 17, No. 2, pp. 199–236.

[32] Levy, D. & Schuck, E. (2005), 'The influence of clients on valuations: the clients' perspective', *Journal of Property Investment & Finance*, Vol. 23, No. 2, pp. 182–201. https://doi.org/10.1108/14635780510584364.

[33] Lind, H. & Nyström, J. (2011), 'The Explanation of Incomplete Contracts in Mainstream Contract Theory: A Critique of the Distinction between "Observable" and "Verifiable"', *Evolutionary and Institutional Economics Review*, Vol. 7, No. 2, pp. 279–293.

[34] McAllister, P. (2020), 'Creating operational alpha? Operating models for real estate management', *Property Management*, Vol. 38, No. 4, pp. 565–583. https://doi.org/10.1108/PM-02-2020-0009.

[35] Mas-Colell, A., Whinston, M. D. & Green, J. R. (1995), 'Microeconomic Theory', *Oxford University Press*.

[36] Mielke, J. & Steudle, G. A. (2018), 'Green Investment and Coordination Failure: An Investor's Perspective', *Ecological Economics*, Vol. 150, pp. 88–95. https://doi.org/10.1016/j.ecolecon.2018.03.018.

[37] Milgrom, P. & Roberts, J. (1992), 'Economics, Organization and Management', *Prentice Hall*.

[38] Morgenstern, O. & von Neumann, J. (1944), 'The Theory of Games and Economic Behavior', *Princeton University Press*.

[39] Newbold, P, Carlson, W. & Thorne, B. (2019), 'Statistics for Business and Economics', *Pearson*.

[40] Olander, S. & Atkin, B. L. (2010), 'Stakeholder management – the gains and pains', In *Construction Stakeholder Management*, 15, (Eds. Chinyio E. & Olomolaiye, P.), pp. 266–275, *Wiley-Blackwell*.

[41] Olsen, T. E. & Osmundsen, P. (2005), 'Sharing of endogenous risk in construction', *Journal of Economic Behavior & Organization*, Vol. 58, pp. 511–526.

[42] Páez-Pérez, D. & Sánchez-Silva, M. (2016), 'A dynamic principal-agent framework for modeling the performance of infrastructure', *European Journal of Operational Research*, Vol. 254, No. 2, pp. 576–594.

[43] Perloff, J. M. (2022), 'Microeconomics: Theory and Applications with Calculus', 5th Ed., *Pearson*.

[44] Pfrang, D. C. & Wittig, S. (2008), 'Negotiating office lease contracts: From a game-theoretic towards a behavioural view', *Journal of European Real Estate Research*, Vol 1, No. 1, pp. 88–105. https://doi.org/10.1108/17539260810891514.

[45] Rodrik, D. (2015) 'Economics Rules', *Oxford University Press*.

[46] Schieg, M. (2008), 'Strategies for avoiding asymmetric information in construction project management, *Journal of Business Economics and Management*, Vol. 9, No. 1, pp. 47–51.

[47] Spence, M. (1973), 'Job Market Signaling', *The Quarterly Journal of Economics*, Vol. 87, No. 3, pp. 355–374.

[48] Stiglitz, J. E. (1975), 'The Theory of "Screening," Education, and the Distribution of Income', *American Economic Review*, Vol. 65, No. 3, pp. 283–300.

[49] Thaler, R. H. (1992), 'The winner's curse: paradoxes and anomalies of economics life', *Princeton University Press*.

[50] Tirole, J. (1994), 'The Theory of Industrial Organization', *The MIT Press*.

[51] U.S. Department of Justice and the Federal Trade Commission (2010), 'Horizontal Merger Guidelines'.

[52] Varian, H. R. (1992), 'Microeconomic Analysis', 3rd Ed., *W. W. Norton*.

[53] Varian, H. R. (2020), 'Intermediate Microeconomics: A Modern Approch', 9th Ed., *W. W. Norton*.

[54] Watson, J. (2013), 'Strategy: an introduction to game theory', 3rd Ed., *W. W. Norton*.

Index

Printed in the United States
by Baker & Taylor Publisher Services